REFACTORING
WORKBOOK

REFACTORING WORKBOOK

William C. Wake

✦▾Addison-Wesley

Boston • San Francisco • New York • Toronto • Montreal
London • Munich • Paris • Madrid
Cape Town • Sydney • Tokyo • Singapore • Mexico City

The publisher offers discounts on this book when ordered in quantity for bulk purchases and special sales. For more information, please contact:

U.S. Corporate and Government Sales
(800) 382-3419
corpsales@pearsontechgroup.com

For sales outside of the U.S., please contact:

International Sales
(317) 581-3793
international@pearsontechgroup.com

Visit Addison-Wesley on the Web: www.awprofessional.com

Library of Congress Cataloging-in-Publication Data
Wake, William C.
    Refactoring workbook / William C. Wake.
        p. cm.
    Includes bibliographical references and index.
    ISBN 0-321-10929-5 (pbk.)
    1. Software refactoring. I. Title.

    QA76.76.R42W35 2003
    005.1'6—dc22

                                       2003057903

Pearson Education, Inc.
Rights and Contracts Department
75 Arlington Street, Suite 300
Boston, MA 02116
Fax: (617) 848-7047
ISBN: 0321109295

Text printed on recycled paper

1 2 3 4 5 6 7 8 9 10

First printing, August, 2003

Booker Tyler Wake, 1913–2002
A truly great uncle

CONTENTS

PREFACE   *xiii*

1 ROADMAP   *1*

Overview   *1*

Section 1: Smells within Classes   *2*

Section 2: Smells between Classes   *2*

Section 3: Programs to Refactor   *2*

A Word on the Challenges   *3*

SECTION   1   ■   SMELLS WITHIN CLASSES   5

2 THE REFACTORING CYCLE   *7*

What Is Refactoring?   *7*

Smells Are Problems   *8*

The Refactoring Cycle   *9*

When Are We Done?   *9*

Inside a Refactoring   *12*

Challenges   *15*

Conclusion   *15*

3 MEASURED SMELLS   *17*

Smells Covered   *17*

Comments   *18*

Long Method   *20*

Large Class   *25*

Long Parameter List   *30*

More Challenges   *32*

Conclusion   *33*

INTERLUDE 1   SMELLS AND REFACTORINGS   35

4 NAMES   *39*

Smells Covered   *40*

Type Embedded in Name (Including Hungarian)   *40*

Uncommunicative Name   *41*

Inconsistent Names   *42*

5 UNNECESSARY COMPLEXITY   *45*

Smells Covered   *45*

Dead Code   *45*

Speculative Generality   *46*

INTERLUDE 2   INVERSES   *49*

6 DUPLICATION   *51*

Smells Covered   *52*

Magic Number   *52*

Duplicated Code   *53*

Alternative Classes with Different Interfaces   *54*

Challenges   *55*

7 CONDITIONAL LOGIC   *63*

Smells Covered   *63*

Null Check   *63*

Complicated Boolean Expression   *65*

Special Case   *67*

Simulated Inheritance (Switch Statement)   *68*

INTERLUDE 3   DESIGN PATTERNS   *71*

**SECTION   2   ■   SMELLS BETWEEN
                    CLASSES   73**

8 DATA   *75*

Smells Covered   *75*

Primitive Obsession   *75*

Data Class   *79*

Data Clump   *83*

Temporary Field   85

9 INHERITANCE   87

Smells Covered   87
Refused Bequest   87
Inappropriate Intimacy (Subclass Form)   90
Lazy Class   90

10 RESPONSIBILITY   93

Smells Covered   93
Feature Envy   93
Inappropriate Intimacy (General Form)   95
Message Chains   96
Middle Man   97
Challenges   98

11 ACCOMMODATING CHANGE   103

Smells Covered   103
Divergent Change   103
Shotgun Surgery   107
Parallel Inheritance Hierarchies   108
Combinatorial Explosion   109

12 LIBRARY CLASSES   111

Smells Covered   111
Incomplete Library Class   111
Challenges   112

INTERLUDE 4   GEN-A-REFACTORING   117

SECTION   3 ■ PROGRAMS TO REFACTOR   119

13 A DATABASE EXAMPLE   121

Course.java (Online at www.xp123.com/rwb)   122
Offering.java   124
Schedule.java   126
Report.java   129

TestSchedule.java   131
TestReport.java   134

14 A SIMPLE GAME *141*

Development Episodes   147

15 CATALOG *151*

Introduction   151
Path 1: Catalog.itemsMatching(query)   152
Path 2: Query.matchesIn(catalog)   155
Path 3: Process(catalog.data, query.data)   156
Conclusion   157

16 PLANNING GAME SIMULATOR *159*

Part 1: Original Code   160
Code (Online at www.xp123.com/rwb)   160
Table.java   160
Background.java   164
Card.java   165
Challenges   168
Part 2: Redistributing Features   170
Five Whys   172
Removing Duplication, Selection Troubles, and a Few
    Burrs   173
Part 3: Pushing the Code Further   176

17 WHERE TO GO FROM HERE *181*

Books   181
Admonitions   181
Build Refactoring into Your Practice   181
Build Testing into Your Practice   181
Get Help from Others   182
Exercises to Try   182
Smell Scavenger Hunt/Smell of the Week   182
Re-Refactor   182
Just Refactor   182
Inhale/Exhale   182

Defactoring/Malfactoring   *182*

Refactoring Kata   *183*

Web Sites   *183*

SECTION 4 ■ APPENDIXES 185

A ANSWERS TO SELECTED QUESTIONS *187*

B JAVA REFACTORING TOOLS *219*

C INVERSES FOR REFACTORINGS *221*

D KEY REFACTORINGS *223*

BIBLIOGRAPHY *227*

INDEX *229*

PREFACE

What Is Refactoring?

Refactoring is the art of *improving the design of existing code*. Refactoring provides us with ways to recognize problematic code and gives us recipes for improving it.

What Are the Goals of This Book?

This book is a workbook designed to help you

- Practice recognizing the most important *smells* (i.e., problems)
- Apply the most important refactoring techniques
- Think more about how to create great code
- Have fun!

To a smaller extent, this book is a reference book with

- A *smell finder* inside the covers
- A standard format for describing smells
- An appendix listing Java tools supporting refactoring
- An appendix showing key refactorings

Who Is This Book For?

Refactoring being a technique for code, this book then is especially intended for practicing programmers who write and maintain code.

Students can also benefit from refactoring, although I'd expect they'd see the value only after they've had a chance to develop medium-sized or larger programs or had to work in teams (this probably applies to juniors, seniors, and graduate students).

What Background Do You Need?

It would be helpful to have the book, *Refactoring: Improving the Design of Existing Code*, by Martin Fowler et al. (or at least to have access to the *www.refactoring.com* Web site) for its catalog of refactorings. (You can read my book and *Refactoring* at the same time.) Martin and his colleagues have worked out step-by-step instructions for many refactorings, and I will not repeat those in this book. Furthermore, they've provided a fully worked-out example, along with a lot of good discussion and background material. Someone determined to get through this book without that one could probably do it, but I wouldn't recommend it.

The examples in this book are written in Java. This is not because it's the easiest language to refactor, but because it's popular, and the best Java development environments provide automated refactoring support. A C# or C++ programmer has enough reading knowledge of Java to make sense of most of the questions. However, in later parts of the book, you will modify, test, and run larger programs, and this could be problematic for programmers using languages other than Java.

The book *Design Patterns,* by Gamma et al., describes patterns as "targets for refactoring." It would be helpful to have some familiarity with the ideas in that book because I freely refer to the patterns it mentions. If you're not yet familiar with *Design Patterns,* let me recommend Steve Metsker's book, *Design Patterns Java Workbook,* as well.

How to Use This Book

Solving a problem is more challenging than recognizing a solution. There are answers to some problems in the back of the book, but you'll learn more if you try the problems before peeking at the answers. If you work through the problems, you'll probably even find that you disagree with me on some answers. That will be more fun for all of us than if you just look at my answers and nod.

I think it's more fun to work with others (either a partner or in a small group), but I recognize that isn't always possible.

The later (longer) examples need to be done at a computer. Looking for problems, and figuring out how to solve them, is different when you're looking at a program in your environment.

Can I Contact the Author?

Sure: *William.Wake@acm.org.*

I have a Web site as well: *www.xp123.com.* Its focus is extreme programming (XP), and refactoring is an important part of that. Refactoring (and this book) has its own corner: *www.xp123.com/rwb.*

I'm interested in your experience with these exercises, as well as with refactoring in general, so please feel free to write.

Acknowledgments

One of the challenges of writing a book is that it's hard to effectively acknowledge the many people who have helped you. You know you're forgetting names, and you know that the book could be even better if only you could take all of their advice.

Many people offered advice on various drafts of or exercises in this book, including Philippe Antras, Ron Crocker, Sven Gorts, Harris Kirk, Tom Kubit, Paul Michali (who provided one of the examples), Edmund Schweppe, Steve Wake, Robert Wenner, and others I know I've omitted. Sven Gorts and Tom Kubit get special mention, as they both gave me particularly extensive feedback and advice. Ann Anderson, Ken Auer, and Don Wells reviewed the manuscript for the publisher.

My programmer friends at Gene Codes Corporation (working for Howard Cash) worried that anything they did would become fodder for another example. (Their code isn't in here, but they all helped me think about what I was trying to communicate, and each gave me advice on at least some examples.) Thanks to Lucy Hadden, Jonathan Hoyle, Anna Khizhnyak, Tom Kubit, Greg Poth, and Dave Relyea.

This book owes obvious debt to the prior work of Martin Fowler and Kent Beck. Their encouragement has been as important. The format of the book is inspired by Steve Metsker's *Design Patterns Java Workbook*; discussions with him have been very helpful.

At Addison-Wesley/Prentice Hall, I need to thank Mike Hendrickson, Ross Venables, Anne Garcia, Michelle Vincenti, and especially my editor, Paul Petralia. Don MacLaren and Ruth Frick of BooksCraft improved the text considerably. There are many others who put a lot of work into turning the manuscript into a book; I don't know their names, but I appreciate what they do.

Pearson allowed me to use information from other books:

- Beck, EXTREME PROGRAMMING EXPLAINED: EMBRACING CHANGE, page 57, © 2000 by Kent Beck. Reprinted by permission of Pearson Education, Inc. Publishing as Pearson Addison Wesley.
- Fowler, REFACTORING: IMPROVING THE DESIGN OF EXISTING CODE, inside front cover (List of Refactorings); inside back cover (Smell-Common Refactorings), © 1999 by Addison Wesley Longman, Inc. Reprinted by permission of Pearson Education, Inc. Publishing as Pearson Addison Wesley.
- Gamma/Helm/Johnson/Vlissides, DESIGN PATTERNS: ELEMENTS OF REUSABLE OBJECT-ORIENTED SOFTWARE, pp. viii and ix (patterns list from the Table of Contents) © 1995 by Addison-Wesley Publishing Company. Reprinted by permission of Pearson Education, Inc. Publishing as Pearson Addison Wesley.
- Wake, EXTREME PROGRAMMING EXPLORED, pp.24–25, © 2002 Pearson Education, Inc. Reprinted by permission of Pearson Education, Inc. Publishing as Pearson Addison Wesley.

Finally, no acknowledgment would be complete without thanking my family. They don't just tolerate my writing, but give me encouragement, support, and love. Who could ask for more?

1

ROADMAP

Overview

This book is divided into three sections. Section 1 focuses on *smells* (problems) that occur *within* classes. Section 2 focuses on smells that occur *between* classes. Section 3 provides large programs for practicing refactoring in a variety of domains. Sprinkled among these sections, there are what I have called interludes—brief excursions into analyzing the refactoring catalog in *Refactoring: Improving the Design of Existing Code*, by Martin Fowler et al. (hereafter referred to as Fowler's *Refactoring*), or the patterns in *Design Patterns* by Erich Gamma et al. (similarly referred to as Gamma's *Design Patterns*).

In the first two sections, the chapters consist mostly of smells (warning signs of potential problems) and challenges (exercises). I've used a standard format for describing smells:

Smell—its name

Symptoms—cues that help you spot it

Causes—notes on how it might happen

What to do—possible refactorings

Payoff—the ways your code will improve

Contraindications—when not to fix it

This should help keep the smell pages useful for reference even when you've finished the challenges.

The challenges vary; some ask you to analyze code, others to assess a situation, still others to revise code. Code-based exercises have their code online at *www.xp123.com/rwb*.

Not all challenges are equally easy. The harder ones have "(Challenging)" between the challenge number and title; you'll see that these often have room for variation in their answers. Most exercises have solutions (or ideas to help you find solutions) in Appendix A. The later (code-based) exercises tend not to have answers, because they're asking you to modify programs.

Section 1: Smells within Classes

In Chapter 2, we'll take a brief look at the refactoring cycle. Chapter 3 is about measurable smells—those indicated by simple *length* metrics. Chapter 4 looks at how names contribute to the simplicity and comprehensibility of code. Chapter 5 considers the problem of unnecessary code.

The topic of Chapter 6—duplication—is, in many ways, the core smell we need to be sensitive to. Many of the other smells can be regarded as special cases of duplication.

Section 1 closes with Chapter 7, a look at conditional logic: how the expressions used by conditional and loop statements can be made more clear.

Section 2: Smells between Classes

Data in classes can sometimes represent missing objects; Chapter 8 considers this problem.

Chapter 9 looks at the balance of responsibility between superclasses and subclasses, while Chapter 10 goes on to consider the balance of responsibility between other classes. The smells in Chapter 10 must sometimes trade off against each other as we decide how best to connect objects.

Some duplication becomes most obvious when you try to change things, as you will see in Chapter 11. Chapter 12 closes out this section by looking at some challenges in using library classes.

Section 3: Programs to Refactor

The last section of this book provides you with programs to refactor.

Chapter 13 is a simple course registration system that uses a database. Refactoring code and databases together is an emerging area of study; we'll find plenty of duplication to fix in the code.

Chapter 14 looks at a simple game. Even a small program embodies a lot of decisions and has room for a number of smells. We'll touch on test-driven development as well.

Chapter 15 considers some challenges in balancing responsibility. We'll use refactoring to explore three different approaches to an online catalog. Even with only three or four classes, we can arrive at radically different solutions.

Chapter 16 tackles a graphical user interface (GUI). This example demonstrates a common problem: You want unit tests so you can safely refactor, but you need to refactor to make the code testable.

Finally, Chapter 17 suggests some exercises that you can apply in your own work and provides suggestions for further reading.

A Word on the Challenges

There's an easy way to do the exercises: Read the question, look up the answer, and nod because it sounds plausible. This may lead you to my insights.

Then there's a harder but far better way to do the exercises: Read the question, solve the problem, and only then look up the answer. This has a much better chance of leading you to your own insights.

Particularly for the code you're asked to modify, hands-on practice will help you learn more. Refactoring is a skill that requires practice.

Good luck!

SECTION 1

SMELLS WITHIN CLASSES

THE REFACTORING CYCLE

In this chapter, we'll look at refactoring at two levels:

1. The broad cycle of identifying and fixing problems
2. The types of manipulations you make in individual refactorings

What Is Refactoring?

Refactoring is the art of safely improving the design of existing code. This has a few implications:

- *Refactoring does not include just any changes in a system.* Changes that represent design improvements or add new functionality are not all considered to be refactoring. While refactoring can be part of the process used to create new code, it's not the part that adds new features. For example, *Extreme Programming*, or XP, (described in Kent Beck's *Extreme Programming Explained: Embrace Change*) uses test-driven development, which consists of writing a test, then writing new code to introduce new features, and, finally, refactoring to improve the design.
- *Refactoring is not rewriting from scratch.* While there are times when it's better to start fresh, refactoring changes the balance point, making it possible to improve code rather than take the risk of rewriting it. Sven Gorts points out (private communication) that refactoring preserves the knowledge embedded in the existing code.
- *Refactoring is not just any restructuring intended to improve code.* What distinguishes our definition from this is the idea that refactorings strive to be *safe* transformations. Even *big* refactorings that change large amounts of code

are divided into smaller, safe refactorings. (In the best case, refactorings are so well defined that they can be automated.) We won't regard a change as refactoring if it leaves the code not working (that is, not passing its tests) for longer than a working session.

- *Refactoring changes the balance point between up-front design and emergent design.* Up-front design is design done in advance of implementation; emergent design is design intertwined with implementation. The trade-off between up-front and emergent design hinges on how well we can anticipate problems or assess them in code, and whether it's easier to *design and then translate to code* or *to code and then improve.* Refactoring lowers the cost and risk of the emergent approach. (Reasonable people will disagree on where the line is, but I think all will agree that it shifts.)
- *Refactorings can be small or large.* Many refactorings are small. Ideally, small refactorings are applied "mercilessly" enough that large refactorings are rarely needed. Even when applying large-scale refactorings, the approach is not *no new features for six months while we refactor,* but rather, *refactor as we go, and keep the system running at all times.*

Smells Are Problems

Smells (especially *code smells*) are warning signs about potential problems in code. Not all smells indicate a problem, but most are worthy of a look and a decision.

Some people dislike the term *smell,* and prefer to talk about *potential problems* or *flaws,* but I think smell is a good metaphor. Think about what happens when you open a fridge that has a few things going bad inside. Some smells will be strong, and it will be obvious what to do about them. Other smells will be subtler; you won't be sure if the problem is caused by the leftover peas or maybe that Kung Pao chicken. Some food in the fridge may be bad without having a particularly bad smell. Code smells seem like that to me: Some are obvious, some aren't. Some mask other problems. Some go away unexpectedly when you fix something else.

Smells usually describe localized problems. It would be nice if people could find problems easily across a whole system. But humans aren't so good at that job; local smells work with our tendency to consider only the part we're looking at right now.

The Refactoring Cycle

There's a basic pattern for refactoring:

> **The Refactoring Cycle**
> Start with a working program.
> While smells remain:
> - Choose the worst smell.
> - Select a refactoring that will address the smell.
> - Apply the refactoring.

We try to select refactorings that improve the code in each trip through the cycle. Because none of the steps change the program's observable behavior, the program remains in a working state. Thus, the cycle improves code but retains behavior. The trickiest part of the whole process is identifying the smell, and that's why the bulk of this book emphasizes that topic.

Is this approach to refactoring guaranteed to get to the ideal design for a problem? Unfortunately, no, as there's no guarantee that you can reach a global maximum by looking at local properties. But it's easier to get design insights that transform a solution when the code is as clean as possible.

Refactoring is like crossing a stream. One way to cross a stream is to take a running leap and hope for the best. The refactoring way is to find stepping stones and to cross the stream by stepping on one stone at a time.

When you start refactoring, it's best to start with the easy stuff (for example, breaking up large routines or renaming things for clarity). You'll find that this lets you see and fix the remaining problems more easily.

When Are We Done?

One approach is to seek the simplest design. Kent Beck has identified four rules for simple design; if your code violates these rules (which are in priority order), then you have a problem to address.

Simple Design

1. Runs all the tests.
2. Has no duplicated logic. Be wary of hidden duplication like parallel class hierarchies.
3. States every intention important to the programmers.
4. Has the fewest possible classes and methods.

—Beck, *Extreme Programming Explained*, p. 57

A shorthand name for these rules is OAOO, which stands for *once and only once*. The code has to state something once so that it can pass its tests and communicate the programmer's understanding and intent. And it should say things only once, i.e., with no duplication.

It's hard to clean up code that hasn't been kept clean; few teams can afford to turn the lights out for months on a quest for perfection. But we can learn to make our code better during development, and we can add a little energy each time we're working in an area.

EXTREME PROGRAMMING (XP) AND REFACTORING

Extreme Programming is an *agile* software development method, characterized by a particular planning style, a team focus, and programming through tests and refactoring. While refactoring has been around longer, there's a cluster of people—including Kent Beck, Ward Cunningham, Martin Fowler, and Ralph Johnson—who have been working in the areas of object-oriented development, patterns, refactoring, and other related ideas.

Programming in XP is built around three things: an ethos of simple design, test-first programming, and refactoring. Test-first programming is an approach that says, "Write a test, see it fail, write code, see the test pass." When you put all of these together, you get what is now called *test-driven development*. See *Test-Driven Development: A Practical Guide* by Dave Astels and *Test-Driven Development: By Example* by Kent Beck for a deeper description of this technique.

I'm a fan of the test-driven approach (and XP, for that matter), but the discipline of refactoring doesn't require it. However, code created this way will typically have fewer errors and will need less of the big refactoring that typical code requires. In particular, the bigger examples in the last half of this book would be much smaller and less smelly if they'd been done using test-driven development.

THE ENVIRONMENT FOR REFACTORING

Refactoring can be done with just a simple text editor, but refactoring is easier and safer with a supportive environment.

Team or Partner: For nontrivial decisions about code, it's helpful to have more than one person considering the problem. A team can often generate ideas better than one person alone: Different people have different experiences and different exposure to different parts of the system.

Tests: Even though refactorings are designed to be safe, it's possible to make a mistake in applying them. By having a test suite that is run before and after refactoring, you help ensure that you change the design of your code, not its effects.

What if you don't have tests? Then add them, at least to the areas affected by the refactoring. Sometimes this is tricky—you may be unable to test effectively without changing the design, and yet it's unsafe to change the design without tests. And areas that are tricky to test often indicate other problems in the design.

"If you want to refactor, the essential precondition is having solid tests."

—Martin Fowler, *Refactoring,* p. 89

Testing Framework: The JUnit test framework (*www.junit.org*) has become a standard. The later examples use it. Test classes extend the TestCase class, and they contain methods whose names start with the word *test*. The framework provides a number of *assert* methods that let you verify the code's behavior. It also comes with a test runner that can run a suite of tests.

CRC Cards or UML Sketches: Refactoring doesn't mean eliminating design. Sometimes you may hold a Class-Responsibility-Collaborator (CRC) card session or draw Unified Modeling Language (UML) sketches to compare alternatives for refactoring.

Configuration Management/Version Control: This can range from Undo to a full-fledged configuration management system. If you make a mistake while refactoring, you'd like to be able to return to the last *known good* point. Alternatively, you may want to apply a refactoring, but you may not be sure if the result will be an improvement. It's helpful to be able to try it and then decide whether to keep the result.

Sophisticated Integrated Development Environment (IDE): Simple, but powerful, languages such as Smalltalk and Lisp have had refactoring support available in their environments for a number of years. Java has had such support only for the last year or two, and refactoring support is just now beginning to show up for C#. The user still has to decide which refactoring to apply, but the tool removes a lot of the error-prone tedium.

Inside a Refactoring

One of the defining aspects of refactoring is the focus on safe transformations. We'll walk through a simple refactoring. Along the way we'll derive some guidelines that will help us better understand how refactorings work.

Consider the refactoring *Encapsulate Field*. Its goal is to make clients of an object use methods to access a field rather than having them access the field directly:

```
public String name;
    →
private String name;
public String getName() {return name;}
public void setName(String newName) {name = newName;}
```

Martin Fowler's catalog tells us to

1. Create getters and setters for the field.
2. Locate all references; replace accesses with calls to the getter and changes to the field with calls to the setter.
3. Compile and test after changing each reference.
4. Declare the field as private.
5. Compile and test.

Refactoring is a step-by-step process. The steps are smaller than people typically expect. Most refactorings tend to take from a minute to an hour to apply; the average is probably five to ten minutes. So, if a refactoring takes a few minutes, the steps are even smaller.

Refactoring works in tiny steps.

Initially, we have:

```
public class Person {public String name;}
```

The test client looks like this:

```
Person person;
person.name = "Bob Smith";
assertEquals("Bob Smith", person.name);
```

Step 1: Create getter and setter methods.

```
public class Person {
    public String name;
    public String getName() {return name;}
```

```
    public void setName(String newName) {name = newName;}
}
```

Note that the client is unchanged: no code is calling these new methods yet.

Step 2: Find all clients; replace references with calls. Do this one at a time.

One way to find those references is to temporarily make the field private; if you do this, put it back to public scope before changing the clients so you don't break any clients.

In many refactorings, the compiler will tell you if things are going right. For example, suppose you're using *Hide Method* to make a public method be private. When you change the visibility keyword and recompile, you get a warning that some client is still using the method. Because the warning is at compile-time instead of an error at run-time, you're protected while you refactor.

The compiler talks to you.

Assignment—

```
person.name = "Bob Smith";
```

becomes

```
person.setName("Bob Smith");
```

Step 3: Compile and test.

Even though refactorings have the goal of having an improved system at the end of the refactoring, many of them have *bases*, *safe points*, or *interruption points* along the way (think of bases in baseball or the children's game of tag; they may not be the ultimate destination, but at least you can't get tagged while you're on the base). Since it embodies two different approaches in the midst of refactoring, the system is not as clean as it will be in the end, but we can stop, run the tests, and make sure we're OK so far.

Most refactorings have built-in *bases*.

I imagine holding my breath while the system is in an unsafe state and then letting it go when the tests run correctly. This mild tension and release feels so much better than the feeling you get where you're halfway through one thing and you realize you want to do something else before you finish, and so on, and so on, until you're juggling five balls instead of one.

Large refactorings use this idea of bases as well. It's even more important there. If it will take months to clean out the remnants of some decision, we must have safe points along the way.

Step 2: Replace the other reference.

Reference—

```
assertEquals("Bob Smith", person.name);
```

becomes

```
assertEquals("Bob Smith", person.getName());
```

Step 3: Compile and test.

If we absolutely had to, we could stop after either occurrence of step 3 and still be safe. The code would be worse than when we started in one sense: It uses two inconsistent approaches to access the field. Nevertheless, it is progress toward a better approach.

Step 4: Once all clients are changed, make the field private.

```
public class Person {
    private String name;
    public String getName() {return name;}
    public void setName(String newName) {name = newName;}
}
```

Step 5: Compile and test one last time.

Again, we're safe, and the field is completely encapsulated.

Challenges

EXERCISE 1   Small Steps.

> **Pick a refactoring and identify a place where the approach builds in small steps even though larger steps could work.**
>
> ■ *See Appendix A for solutions.*

EXERCISE 2   Simple Design.

> **A. Justify each of Beck's rules for simple design.**
> **B. Why are these rules in priority order? Can you find an example where communication overrides avoidance of duplication?**
>
> ■ *See Appendix A for solutions.*

Conclusion

As you use refactorings, and as you develop new ones, use them in such a way that the system moves from good state to good state. Prefer a *small steps but safer* approach to a *fast but not always safe* approach when you refactor. Keep the refactoring cycle in mind.

3

MEASURED SMELLS

The smells in this chapter are similar. They're dead easy to detect. They're objective (once you decide on a way to count and a maximum acceptable score). They're odious.

And, they're common.

You can think of these smells as being caught by a software metric. Each metric tends to catch different aspects of why code isn't as good as it could be. Some metrics measure variants of code length; others try to measure the connections between methods or objects; others measure a distance from an ideal.

Most metrics seem to correlate with length, so I tend to worry about size first (usually noticeable as a Large Class or Long Method). But if a metric is easy to compute, I'll use it as an indicator that some section of code deserves a closer look.

Metrics are indicators, not absolutes. It's very easy to get into the trap of *making numbers* without addressing the total complexity. So don't refactor just for a better number; make sure it really improves your code.

Smells Covered

- Comments
- Long Method
- Large Class
- Long Parameter List

Comments

Symptoms

- Comment symbols (// or /*) appear in the code. (Some IDEs help by color coding different types of comments.)

Causes

Comments may be present for the best of reasons: The author realizes that something isn't as clear as it could be and adds a comment.

Some comments are particularly helpful:

- Those that tell why something is done a particular way (or why it wasn't)
- Those that cite algorithms that are not obvious (where a simpler algorithm won't do)

Other comments can be reflected just as well in the code itself. For example, the goal of a routine can often be communicated as well through the routine's name as it can through a comment.

What to Do

- When a comment explains a block of code, you can often use *Extract Method* to pull the block out into a separate method. The comment will often suggest a name for the new method.
- When a comment explains what a method does (better than the method's name!), use *Rename Method* using the comment as the basis of the new name.
- When a comment explains preconditions, consider using *Introduce Assertion* to replace the comment with code.

Payoff

Improves communication. May expose duplication.

Contraindications

Don't delete comments that are pulling their own weight.

EXERCISE 3 Comments.

Consider this code. (Online at *www.xp123.com/rwb*)

Matcher.java

```java
public class Matcher {
    public Matcher() {}
    public boolean match(int[] expected, int[] actual,
        int clipLimit, int delta)
    {

        // Clip "too-large" values
        for (int i = 0; i < actual.length; i++)
            if (actual[i] > clipLimit)
                actual[i] = clipLimit;

        // Check for length differences
        if (actual.length != expected.length)
            return false;

        // Check that each entry within expected +/- delta
        for (int i = 0; i < actual.length; i++)
            if (Math.abs(expected[i] - actual[i]) > delta)
                return false;

        return true;
    }
}
```

MatcherTest.java

```java
import junit.framework.TestCase;

public class MatcherTest extends TestCase {
    public MatcherTest(String name) {super(name);}

    public void testMatch() {
        Matcher matcher = new Matcher();

        int[] expected = new int[] {10, 50, 30, 98};
        int clipLimit = 100;
        int delta = 5;

        int[] actual = new int[] {12, 55, 25, 110};

        assertTrue(matcher.match(expected, actual, clipLimit, delta));

        actual = new int[] {10, 60, 30, 98};
        assertTrue(!matcher.match(expected, actual, clipLimit, delta));
```

EXERCISE 3 Comments. (Continued)

```
        actual = new int[] {10, 50, 30};
        assertTrue(!matcher.match(expected, actual, clipLimit, delta));
        }
}
```

    A. Use *Extract Method* to make the comments in `match()` redundant.

    B. Can everything important about the code be communicated using the code alone? Or do comments have a place?

    C. Find some code you wrote recently. Odds are good that you commented it. Can you eliminate the need for some of those comments by making the code reflect your intentions more directly?

                                              ■ *See Appendix A for solutions.*

Long Method

Symptoms

- Large number of lines. (I'm immediately suspicious of any method with more than 5 to 10 lines.)

Causes

I think of it as the *Columbo syndrome*. Columbo was the detective who always had "just one more thing." A method starts down a path and, rather than break the flow or identify the helper classes, the author adds one more thing. Code is often easier to write than it is to read, so there's a temptation to write blocks that are too big.

What to Do

- Use *Extract Method* to break up the method into smaller pieces. Look for comments or white space delineating interesting blocks. You want to extract methods that are semantically meaningful, not just introduce a function call every seven lines.
- You may find other refactorings (those that clean up straight-line code, conditionals, and variable usage) helpful before you even begin splitting up the method.

Payoff

Improves communication. May expose duplication. Often helps new classes and abstractions emerge.

Discussion

- People are sometimes worried about the performance hit from increasing the number of method calls, but most of the time this is a nonissue. By getting the code as clean as possible before worrying about performance, you have the opportunity to gain big insights that can restructure systems and algorithms in a way that dramatically increases performance.
- Don't *game* the metrics; the goal of using *Extract Method* is to use it in a way that increases insight.

Contraindications

It may be that a somewhat longer method is just the best way to express something. (Like almost all smells, the length is a warning sign—not a guarantee—of a problem.)

EXERCISE 4   Long Method

Consider this code. (Online at *www.xp123.com/rwb*)

Machine.java

```java
public class Machine {
    String name;
    String location;
    String bin;
```

EXERCISE 4 Long Method (Continued)

```java
    public Machine(String name, String location) {
    this.name = name;
        this.location = location;
    }

    public String take() {
        String result = bin;
        bin = null;
        return result;
    }

    public String bin() {
        return bin;
    }

    public void put(String bin) {
        this.bin = bin;
    }

    public String name() {return name;}
}
```

Robot.java

```java
public class Robot {
    Machine location;
    String bin;

    public Robot() {}

    public Machine location() {return location;}
    public void moveTo(Machine location) {this.location = location;}

    public void pick() {this.bin = location.take();}
    public String bin() {return bin;}

    public void release() {
        location.put(bin);
        bin = null;
    }
}
```

EXERCISE 4 Long Method (Continued)

RobotTest.java

```java
import junit.framework.*;

public class RobotTest extends TestCase{
    public RobotTest(String name) {super(name);}

  public void testRobot() {
        Machine sorter = new Machine("Sorter", "left");
        sorter.put("chips");
        Machine oven = new Machine("Oven", "middle");
        Robot robot = new Robot();

        assertEquals("chips", sorter.bin());
        assertNull(oven.bin());
        assertNull(robot.location());
        assertNull(robot.bin());

        robot.moveTo(sorter);
        robot.pick();
        robot.moveTo(oven);
        robot.release();

        assertNull(robot.bin());
        assertEquals(oven, robot.location());
        assertNull(sorter.bin());
        assertEuals("chips", oven.bin());
    }
}
```

Report.java

```java
import java.util.*;
import java.io.*;

public class Report {
    public static void report(Writer out, List machines, Robot robot)
            throws IOException
    {
        out.write("FACTORY REPORT\n");

        Iterator line = machines.iterator();
        while (line.hasNext()) {
            Machine machine = (Machine) line.next();
            out.write("Machine " + machine.name());
```

EXERCISE 4 Long Method (Continued)

```
            if (machine.bin() != null)
                out.write(" bin=" + machine.bin());
            out.write("\n");
        }
        out.write("\n");

        out.write("Robot");
        if (robot.location() != null)
                out.write(" location=" + robot.location().name());

        if (robot.bin() != null)
            out.write(" bin=" + robot.bin());

        out.write("\n");

        out.write("========\n");
    }
}
```

ReportTest.java

```java
import junit.framework.TestCase;

import java.util.ArrayList;
import java.io.PrintStream;
import java.io.StringWriter;
import java.io.IOException;

public class ReportTest extends TestCase {
    public ReportTest(String name) {super(name);}

    public void testReport() throws IOException {
        ArrayList line = new ArrayList();
        line.add(new Machine("mixer", "left"));

        Machine extruder = new Machine("extruder", "center");
        extruder.put("paste");
        line.add(extruder);

        Machine oven = new Machine("oven", "right");
        oven.put("chips");
        line.add(oven);

        Robot robot = new Robot();
        robot.moveTo(extruder);
        robot.pick();
```

EXERCISE 4   Long Method (Continued)

```
        StringWriter out = new StringWriter();
        Report.report(out, line, robot);

        String expected =
            "FACTORY REPORT\n" +
            "Machine mixer\nMachine extruder\n" +
            "Machine oven bin=chips\n\n" +
            "Robot location=extruder bin=paste\n" +
            "========\n";

        assertEquals(expected, out.toString());
    }
}
```

A. In Report.java, circle four blocks of code to show which functions you might extract in the process of refactoring this code.

B. Rewrite the report() method as four statements, as if you had done *Extract Method* for each block.

C. Does it make sense to extract a one-line method?

D. Long methods are trivially easy to spot, yet they seem to occur often in real code. Why?

■ *See Appendix A for solutions.*

Large Class

Symptoms

- Large number of instance variables
- Large number of methods
- Large number of lines

Causes

Large classes get big a little bit at a time. The author keeps adding just one more capability to a class until eventually it grows too big. Sometimes the problem is a lack of insight into the parts that make up the whole class. In any case, the class represents too many responsibilities folded together.

What to Do

In general, you're trying to break up the class. If the class has Long Methods, address that smell first. To break up the class, three approaches are most common:

- *Extract Class*, if you can identify a new class that has part of this class's responsibilities
- *Extract Subclass,* if you can divide responsibilities between the class and a new subclass
- *Extract Interface,* if you can identify subsets of features that clients use

Sometimes, the class is big because it's a GUI class, and it represents not only the display component, but the model as well. In this case, you can use *Duplicate Observed Data* to help extract a domain class.

Payoff

Improves communication. May expose duplication.

EXERCISE 5   Large Class.

Consider this declaration from the Java libraries:

```
public class JTable extends JComponent
   implements Accessible, CellEditorListener,
     ListSelectionListener, Scrollable,
     TableColumnModelListener, TableModelListener
{
// Constants
public static final int AUTO_RESIZE_ALL_COLUMNS
public static final int AUTO_RESIZE_LAST_COLUMN
public static final int AUTO_RESIZE_NEXT_COLUMN
public static final int AUTO_RESIZE_OFF
public static final int AUTO_RESIZE_SUBSEQUENT_COLUMNS
```

EXERCISE 5 Large Class. (Continued)

```
// Constructors
public JTable()
public JTable(TableModel, TableColumnModel)
public JTable(TableModel, TableColumnModel, ListSelectionModel)
public JTable(int, int)
public JTable(Object[][], Object[][])
public JTable(java.util.Vector, java.util.Vector)


// Methods
public void addColumn(TableColumn column)
public void addColumnSelectionInterval(int start, int finish)
public void addNotify()
public void addRowSelectionInterval(int start, int finish)
public void clearSelection()
public void columnAdded(TableColumnModelEvent event)
public void columnAtPoint(Point p)
public void columnMarginChanged(ChangeEvent event)
public void columnMoved(TableColumnModelEvent event)
public void columnRemoved(TableColumnModelEvent event)
public void columnSelectionChanged(ListSelectionEvent event)
public void convertColumnIndexToModel(int viewColumn)
public void convertColumnIndexToView(int modelColumn)
public void createDefaultColumnsFromModel()
public boolean editCellAt(int row, int column)
public boolean editCellAt(int row, int column, EventObject event)
public void editingCanceled(ChangeEvent event)
public void editingStopped(ChangeEvent event)
public AccessibleContext getAccessibleContext()
public boolean getAutoCreateColumnsFromModel()
public int getAutoResizeMode()
public TableCellEditor getCellEditor()
public TableCellEditor getCellEditor(int row, int column)
public Rectangle getCellRect(int row, int column, boolean includeSpacing)
public boolean getCellSelectionEnabled()
public TableColumn getColumn(Object object)
public Class getColumnClass(int column)
public int getColumnCount()
public TableColumnModel getColumnModel()
public String getColumnName(int column)
public Boolean getColumnSelectionAllowed()
public TableCellEditor getDefaultEditor(Class class)
public TableCellRenderer getDefaultRenderer(Class class)
public int getEditingColumn()
public int getEditingRow()
public Component getEditorComponent()
public Color getGridColor()
public Dimension getIntercellSpacing()
public TableModel getModel()
```

EXERCISE 5   Large Class. (Continued)

```
public Dimension getPreferredScrollableViewportSize()
public int getRowCount()
public int getRowHeight()
public int getRowMargin()
public Boolean getRowSelectionAllowed()

public int getScrollableBlockIncrement(
Rectangle visible, int orientation, int direction)
public Boolean getScrollableTracksViewportHeight()
public Boolean getScrollableTracksViewportWidth()
public int getScrollableUnitIncrement(
Rectangle visible, int orientation, int direction)
public int getSelectedColumn()
public int getSelectedColumnCount()
public int[] getSelectedColumns()
public int getSelectedRow()
public int getSelectedRowCount()
public int[] getSelectedRows()
public Color getSelectionBackground()
public Color getSelectionForeground()
public ListSelectionModel getSelectionModel()
public Boolean getShowHorizontalLines()
public Boolean getShowVerticalLines()
public JTableHeader getTableHeader()
public String getToolTipText(MouseEvent event)
public TableUI getUI()
public String getUIClassID()
public Object getValueAt(int row, int column)
public Boolean isCellEditable(int row, int column)
public Boolean isCellSelected(int row, int column)
public Boolean isColumnSelected(int column)
public Boolean isEditing()
public boolean isManagingFocus()
public Boolean isRowSelected(int row)
public void moveColumn(int column, int newColumn)
public Component prepareEditor(TableCellEditor editor,
 int row, int column)
public Component prepareRenderer(TableCellRenderer renderer,
 int row, int column)
public void removeColumn(TableColumn column)
public void removeColumnSelectionInterval(int column1, int column2)
public void removeEditor()
public void removeRowSelectionInterval(int row1, int row2)
public void reshape(int x, int y, int width, int height)
public int rowAtPoint(Point point)
public void selectAll()
public void setAutoCreateColumnsFromModel(Boolean doAutoCreate)
public void setAutoResizeModel(int mode)
public void setCellEditor(TableCellEditor editor)
```

EXERCISE 5   Large Class. (Continued)

```
public void setCellSelectionEnabled(Boolean maySelect)
public void setColumnModel(TableColumnModel model)
public void setColumnSelectionAllowed(Boolean maySelect)
public void setColumnSelectionInterval(int column1, int column2)
public void setDefaultEditor(Class class, TableCellEditor editor)
public void setDefaultRenderer(Class class, TableCellRenderer renderer)
public void setEditingColumn(int column)
public void setEditingRow(int row)
public void setGridColor(Color color)
public void setIntercellSpacing(Dimention dim)
public void setModel(TableModel model)
public void setPreferredScrollableViewportSize(Dimension dim)
public void setRowHeight(int height)
public void setRowMargin(int margin)
public void setRowSelectionAllowed(Boolean maySelect)
public void setSelectionBackground(Color background)
public void setSelectionForeground(Color foreground)
public void setSelectionMode(int mode)
public void setSelectionModel(ListSelectionModel model)
public void setShowGrid(Boolean showing)
public void setShowHorizontalLines(Boolean b)
public void setShowVerticalLines(Boolean b)
public void setTableHeader(JTableHeader header)
public void setUI(TableUI ui)
public void setValueAt(Object value, int row, int column)
public void sizeColumnsToFit(int resizingColumn)
public void tableChanged(TableModelEvent event)
public void updateUI()
public void valueChanged(ListSelectionEvent)

// plus 22 protected variables

// plus 10 protected methods

// plus 97 methods inherited from JComponent (and fields etc.)

// plus about 35 methods from Container

// plus about 85 methods from Component

// plus 11 methods from Object
}
```

A. Why does this class have so many methods?

EXERCISE 5   Large Class. (Continued)

B. **Go through the methods listed and categorize them into 5 to 10 major areas of responsibility.**

C. **In what ways could the library writers have eliminated some of these methods?**

D. **In Java, Object has 11 methods. In Smalltalk, it has more than 100. Why the difference? Talk to a Smalltalk person and find out why and whether or not this is a smell.**

■ *See Appendix A for solutions.*

Long Parameter List

Symptoms

- A method has more than one or two parameters.

Causes

You might be trying to minimize coupling between objects. Instead of the called object being aware of relationships between classes, you let the caller locate everything; then the method concentrates on what it is being asked to do with the pieces.

Or a programmer generalizes the routine to deal with multiple variations by creating a general algorithm and a lot of *control* parameters.

What to Do

- If the parameter value can be obtained from another object this one already knows, *Replace Parameter with Method*.
- If the parameters come from a single object, try *Preserve Whole Object*.
- If the data is not from one logical object, you still might group them via *Introduce Parameter Object*.

Payoff

Improves communication. May expose duplication. Often reduces size.

Contraindications

- Sometimes, you *want* to avoid a dependency between two classes. For example, the caller may have the dependency, but you don't want to propagate it. Ensure that your changes don't upset this balance.
- Sometimes the parameters have no meaningful grouping—they don't go together.

Notes

This is one of those places where a smell doesn't guarantee a problem. You might smell a Long Parameter List but decide it's right for the situation at hand.

EXERCISE 6   Long Parameter List.

Consider these methods declared in the Java libraries:

From java.swing.CellRendererPane:

```
public void paintComponent(Graphics gr, Component renderer,
    Container parent, int x, int y, int width, int height,
    Boolean shouldValidate)
```

From java.awt.Graphics:

```
public Boolean drawImage(Image image,
    int x1Dest, int y1Dest, int x2Dest, int y2Dest,
    int x1Source, int y1Source, int x2Source, int y2Source,
    Color color, ImageObserver obs)
```

From java.swing.DefaultBoundedRangeModel:

```
public void setRangeProperties(
    int newValue, int newExtent,
    int newMin, int newMax,
    boolean isAdjusting)
```

From java.swing.JOptionPane:

```
public static int showConfirmDialog(Component parent, Object message, String title, int
optionType, int messageType, Icon icon)
```

EXERCISE 6   Long Parameter List. (Continued)

A. For each declaration above, is there any cluster of parameters you might reasonably group into a new object?

B. Why might those signatures have so many parameters?

C. Look back at the JTable declaration (EXERCISE-5, earlier in the chapter). Do you see any clusters of parameters there?

◼ *See Appendix A for solutions.*

More Challenges

EXERCISE 7   Smells and Refactorings.

Consider these smells:

A. Comments

B. Large Class

C. Long Method

D. Long Parameter List

For each refactoring in the following list, write the letter for the smell(s) it might help cure:

___ *Duplicate Observed Data*
___ *Extract Class*
___ *Extract Interface*
___ *Extract Method*
___ *Extract Subclass*
___ *Introduce Assertion*
___ *Introduce Parameter Object*
___ *Preserve Whole Object*
___ *Rename Method*
___ *Replace Parameter with Method*

◼ *See Appendix A for solutions.*

EXERCISE 8 Triggers.

> Consider the smells described in this chapter (Comments, Large Class, Long Method, Long Parameter List).
>
> A. Which of these do you find most often? Which do you create most often?
>
> B. To stop children from sucking their thumbs, some parents put a bad-tasting or spicy solution on the child's thumb. This serves as a trigger that reminds the child not to do that. What triggers can you give yourself to help you recognize when you're just beginning to create one of these smells?
>
> ■ *See Appendix A for solutions.*

Conclusion

The smells in this chapter are the easiest to identify. They're not necessarily the easiest to fix.

There are other metrics that have been applied to software. Many of them are simply refinements of code length. Pay attention when things feel like they're getting too big.

There is not a one-to-one relationship between refactorings and smells; we'll run into the same refactorings again. For example, *Extract Method* is a tool that can fix many problems.

Finally, remember that a smell is an *indication* of a potential problem, not a *guarantee* of an actual problem. You will occasionally find *false positives*—things that smell to you, but are actually better than the alternatives. But most code has plenty of real smells that can keep you busy.

INTERLUDE 1 SMELLS AND REFACTORINGS

The smells (along with the refactorings commonly used to fix them) from Martin Fowler's book *Refactoring* are listed in Table I-1, and the refactorings are listed in Table I-2.

INTERLUDE I1.1

Tally. Put a tally mark by each refactoring for each time a smell references it.

INTERLUDE I1.2

Refactorings that Fix the Most Smells. Which refactorings fix the most smells?

■ *See Appendix A for solution.*

INTERLUDE I1.3

Refactorings Not Mentioned. Which refactorings aren't mentioned by any of the smells? Why not?

■ *See Appendix A for solutions.*

INTERLUDE I1.4

Other Smells. Does this list suggest any other smells you might want to be aware of?

■ *See Appendix A for solutions.*

TABLE I.1   Smells and Their Associated Refactorings (from Fowler's *Refactoring*, back cover)

SMELL	COMMON REFACTORINGS
Alternative Classes with Different Interfaces	Rename Method, Move Method
Comments	Extract Method, Introduce Assertion
Data Class	Move Method, Encapsulate Field, Encapsulate Collection
Data Clump	Extract Class, Introduce Parameter Object, Preserve Whole Object
Divergent Change	Extract Class
Duplicated Code	Extract Method, Extract Class, Pull Up Method, Form Template Method
Feature Envy	Move Method, Move Field, Extract Method
Inappropriate Intimacy	Move Method, Move Field, Change Bidirectional Association to Unidirectional, Replace Inheritance with Delegation, Hide Delegate
Incomplete Library Class	Introduce Foreign Method, Introduce Local Extension
Large Class	Extract Class, Extract Subclass, Extract Interface, Replace Data Value with Object
Lazy Class	Inline Class, Collapse Hierarchy
Long Method	Extract Method, Replace Temp with Query, Replace Method with Method Object, Decompose Conditional
Long Parameter List	Replace Parameter with Method, Introduce Parameter Object, Preserve Whole Object
Message Chains	Hide Delegate
Middle Man	Remove Middle Man, Inline Method, Replace Delegation with Inheritance
Parallel Inheritance Hierarchies	Move Method, Move Field
Primitive Obsession	Replace Data Value with Object, Extract Class, Introduce Parameter Object, Replace Array with Object, Replace Type Code with Class, Replace Type Code with Subclasses, Replace Type Code with State/Strategy
Refused Bequest	Replace Inheritance with Delegation
Shotgun Surgery	Move Method, Move Field, Inline Class
Speculative Generality	Collapse Hierarchy, Inline Class, Remove Parameter, Rename Method
Switch Statements	Replace Conditional with Polymorphism, Replace Type Code with Subclasses, Replace Type Code with State/Strategy, Replace Parameter with Explicit Methods, Introduce Null Object
Temporary Field	Extract Class, Introduce Null Object

TABLE I.2   Refactorings (from Fowler, *Refactoring*, inside front cover)

Add Parameter	Pull Up Constructor Body
Change Bidirectional Association to Unidirectional	Pull Up Field
Change Reference to Value	Pull Up Method
Change Unidirectional Association to Bidirectional	Push Down Field
Change Value to Reference	Push Down Method
Collapse Hierarchy	Remove Assignment to Parameters
Consolidate Conditional Expression	Remove Control Flag
Consolidate Duplicate Conditional Expression	Remove Middle Man
Convert Procedural Design to Objects	Remove Parameter
Decompose Conditional	Remove Setting Method
Duplicate Observed Data	Rename Method
Encapsulate Collection	Replace Array with Object
Encapsulate Downcast	Replace Conditional with Polymorphism
Encapsulate Field	Replace Constructor with Factory Method
Extract Class	Replace Data Value with Object
Extract Hierarchy	Replace Delegation with Inheritance
Extract Interface	Replace Error Code with Exception
Extract Method	Replace Exception with Test
Extract Subclass	Replace Inheritance with Delegation
Extract Superclass	Replace Magic Number with Symbolic Constant
Form Template Method	Replace Method with Method Object
Hide Delegate	Replace Nested Conditional with Guard Clause
Hide Method	Replace Parameter with Explicit Methods
Inline Class	Replace Parameter with Method
Inline Method	Replace Record with Data Class
Inline Temp	Replace Subclass with Fields
Introduce Assertion	Replace Temp with Query
Introduce Explaining Variable	Replace Type Code with Class
Introduce Foreign Method	Replace Type Code with State/Strategy
Introduce Local Extension	Replace Type Code with Subclasses
Introduce Null Object	Self Encapsulate Field
Introduce Parameter Object	Separate Domain from Presentation
Move Field	Split Temporary Variable
Move Method	Substitute Algorithm
Parameterize Method	Tease Apart Inheritance
Preserve Whole Object	

4
NAMES

The creation of a good mental model is one of the key challenges in developing software. There are several tools people use to help with this:

- Project dictionaries
- Domain vocabularies, ontologies, languages
- XP-style metaphors

How we name things is important. Good names perform several functions:

- They provide a vocabulary for discussing our domain.
- They communicate intent.
- They support subtle expectations about how the system works.
- They support each other in a system of names.

It's hard to pick good names, but it's worth the effort. Ward Cunningham describes using a thesaurus to get just the right sense (see *http://c2.com/cgi/wiki?SystemOfNames*).

Some teams have coding standards and naming standards that affect how names are chosen. I generally follow these guidelines:

- Use verbs for manipulators and nouns and/or adjectives for accessors.
- Use the same word for similar things and different words for different things.
- Prefer one-word names.
- Value communication most.

Especially with tool support, it's not that hard to change a name when you realize there's a better one. It's worth investing energy in improving names as you modify code.

Smells Covered

- Type Embedded in Name (including Hungarian)
- Uncommunicative Name
- Inconsistent Names

Type Embedded in Name (Including Hungarian)

Symptoms

- Names are compound words, consisting of a word plus the type of the argument(s). For example, a method addCourse(Course c).
- Names are in Hungarian notation, where the type of an object is encoded into the name; e.g., iCount as an integer member variable.
- Variable names reflect their type rather than their purpose or role.

How It Got This Way

The type may be added in the name of communication. For example, schedule.addCourse(course) might be regarded as more readable than schedule.add(course). (I don't think it is, but some do.)

The embedded type name represents duplication: Both the argument and the name mention the same type. The embedded name can create unnecessary troubles later on. For example, suppose we introduce a parent class for Course to cover both courses and series of courses. Now, all the places that refer to addCourse() have a name that's not quite appropriate. We either change the name at every call site or live with a poor name. Finally, by naming things for the operation alone, we make it easier to see duplication and recognize new abstractions.

Hungarian notation is often introduced as part of a coding standard. In pointer-based languages (like C), it was useful to know that **ppc is in fact a character, but in object-oriented languages it overcouples a name to its type.

Some programmers or teams use a convention where a prefix indicates that something is a member variable (_count or m_count) or that something is a constant (ALL_UPPER_CASE). Again, this adds friction as we change whether something is a local variable, a member, and so on. Aren't there times when we need to know which is which? Sure—and if it's not easy to tell, then it may be a sign that a class is too big. (The idea that these conventions are problematic is not universally agreed to; even the code in Fowler's *Refactoring* uses _member variables.)

What to Do

- *Rename Method* (or field or constant) to a name that communicates intent without being so tied to a type.

Payoff

Improves communication. May make it easier to spot duplication.

Contraindications

Rarely, you might have a class that wants to do the same sort of operation to two different but related types. For example, we might have a Graph class with addPoint() and addLink() methods. If the abstract behavior for the two cases is the same, it may be appropriate to overload the method name (add()).

Sometimes you're using a coding standard that uses typographical conventions to distinguish different classes of variables. You may then value the team's readability of code above the flexibility of *untyped* names, and follow those conventions.

Uncommunicative Name

Symptoms

A name doesn't communicate its intent well enough.

- One- or two-character names
- Names with vowels omitted
- Numbered variables (e.g., pane1, pane2, and so on)
- Odd abbreviations
- Misleading names

Causes

When you first implement something, you have to name things somehow. You give the best name you can think of at the time and move on. Later, you may have an insight that lets you pick a better name.

What to Do

- Use *Rename Method* (or field, constant, etc.) to give it a better name.

Payoff

Improves communication.

Contraindications

Some teams use i/j/k for loop indexes or c for characters; these aren't too confusing if the scope is reasonably short. Similarly, you may occasionally find that numbered variables communicate better.

EXERCISE 9   Names.

Classify these names as embedded type, uncommunicative, or OK.

   ___ addItem(item)

   ___ doIt()

   ___ getNodesArrayList()

   ___ getData()

   ___ makeIt()

   ___ multiplyIntInt(int1, int2)

   ___ processItem()

   ___ sort()

   ___ spin()

■ *See Appendix A for solutions.*

Inconsistent Names

Symptoms

- One name is used in one place, and a different name is used for the same thing somewhere else. For example, you might see add(), store(), put(), and place()for the same basic feature.

Causes

Different people may create the classes at different times. (People may forget to explore the existing classes before adding more.) Occasionally, you'll find people doing this intentionally (but misguidedly) so they can distinguish the names.

What to Do

Pick the best name, and use *Rename Method* (or field, constant, etc.) to give the same name to the same things. Once you've done this, you may find that some classes appear to be more similar than they did before. Look for a duplication smell and eliminate it.

Payoff

Improve communication. May expose duplication.

Notes

The Eiffel language uses a common pool of words for the names of its library features. You can use this technique as inspiration: Look to existing library names for the vocabulary you use.

EXERCISE 10   Critique the Names.

> Which name would you expect to use?
>
> A. To empty a window (onscreen)
>   clear()
>   wash()
>   erase()
>   deleteAll()
>
> B. For a stack
>   add()
>   insert()
>   push()
>   addToFront()

EXERCISE 10   Critique the Names. (Continued)

    C. For an editor (to get rid of the selected text)

        cut()

        delete()

        clear()

        erase()

    D. As part of a file comparison program

        line1.compare(line2)

        line1.equals(line2)

        line1.identicalTo(line2)

        line1.matches(line2)

■ *See Appendix A for solutions.*

EXERCISE 11   XmlEditor.

You have a class XmlEditor. You want to introduce a parent class.

    A. What do you call it?

    B. You want to introduce an interface that the parent will implement. What's a good name?

■ *See Appendix A for solutions.*

5

UNNECESSARY COMPLEXITY

"You aren't gonna need it."–Ron Jeffries

Code is sometimes more complicated than it has to be to solve the problem at hand. There are two causes for this problem:

- Sometimes code gets complicated for historical reasons (e.g., there can be *code rot*—the leftovers from old ways of doing things), but it no longer needs the complexity.
- Another cause of complexity is the practice of overgeneralizing the design. This is often in anticipation of future requirements, or premature performance tuning.

Remove these problems when you run into them. You'll often find that this can lead to further insight and simplification.

Smells Covered

- Dead Code
- Speculative Generality

Dead Code

Symptoms

- A variable, parameter, field, code fragment, method, or class is not used anywhere (perhaps other than in tests).

Causes

- Requirements have changed, or new approaches are introduced, without adequate cleanup.

- Complicated logic results in some combinations of conditions that can't actually happen; you'll see this when simplifying conditionals.

What to Do

- Delete the unused code and any associated tests.

Payoff

Reduces size. Improves communication. Improves simplicity.

Contraindications

- If your application is a framework, you may have elements present to support clients' needs that, strictly speaking, aren't needed by the framework itself. For example, a class may have an empty *hook* method intended to be called by (not-yet-existing) subclasses.

Notes

This smell can be hard to detect without tool support. Once your suspicions are alerted, you can do things like a global search for `new ClassName`.

Speculative Generality

Symptoms

- There are unused classes, methods, fields, parameters, and such. They may have no clients or only tests as clients.
- Code is more complicated than it has to be for the currently implemented requirements.

Causes

The code may be built with the expectation that it will become more useful, but then it never does. When people try to outguess the needs of the code, they often add things for generality or for completeness that end up never being used. Sometimes the code has been used before, but is no longer needed because of new or revised ways of doing things. (*Speculative Generality* may be *Dead Code* created on purpose.)

What to Do

- For an unnecessary class:
  - If parents or children of the class seem like the right place for its behavior, fold it into one of them via *Collapse Hierarchy*.
  - Otherwise, fold its behavior into its caller via *Inline Class*.
- For an unnecessary method, use *Inline Method* or *Remove Method*.
- For an unnecessary field, ensure there are no references and then remove it.
- For an unnecessary parameter, use *Remove Parameter*.

Payoff

Reduces size. Improves communication. Improves simplicity.

Contraindications

- If your application is a framework, you may have elements present to support clients' needs that, strictly speaking, aren't needed by the framework itself. For example, a class may have an empty *hook* method that will be called by (not-yet-existing) subclasses.
- Some elements are used by test methods, but they're exposed as *test probe points* to allow a test to have privileged information about the class. Be careful though—this may indicate that you're missing an abstraction that you could test independently.

EXERCISE 12   Today versus Tomorrow.

To caricaturize the arguments:

XP argues that speculative generality is a smell, and that you aren't going to need it. That is, make your code meet today's requirements, and don't try to anticipate which way tomorrow's requirements will go. (Thus an XP team is more likely to evolve a framework from an application than to build a framework and use it to create an application.)

Another approach is to design for flexibility or to design for generality. This means that you should fully flesh out your classes based on the expected requirements.

EXERCISE 12   Today versus Tomorrow. (Continued)

What are the forces that will help you decide which
approach is better?

Forces that make it better to design for only today's requirements today	Forces that make it better to design for tomorrow's requirements today

■ *See Appendix A for solutions.*

INTERLUDE 2   INVERSES

When we refactor, we're trying to respond to the forces affecting code. Sometimes what was a good change today no longer looks so good tomorrow, and we find ourselves reversing a refactoring.

INTERLUDE I2.1

> Table I-3 presents a list of refactorings. Next to each refactoring, write the name of the refactoring that undoes its effects. (The refactoring and its inverse will both be on the list.)
>
> ■ *See Appendix C for solution.*

TABLE I.3   Refactorings and Their Inverses

REFACTORING	INVERSE
Add Parameter	
Change Bidirectional Association to Unidirectional	
Change Reference to Value	
Change Unidirectional Association to Bidirectional	
Change Value to Reference	
Collapse Hierarchy	
Extract Class	
Extract Method	
Extract Subclass	
Hide Delegate	

TABLE I.3   Refactorings and Their Inverses (Continued)

REFACTORING	INVERSE
Inline Class	
Inline Method	
Inline Temp	
Introduce Explaining Variable	
Move Field	
Move Method	
Parameterize Method	
Pull Up Field	
Pull Up Method	
Push Down Field	
Push Down Method	
Remove Middle Man	
Remove Parameter	
Rename Method	
Replace Delegation with Inheritance	
Replace Inheritance with Delegation	
Replace Parameter with Explicit Methods	
Substitute Algorithm	

6

DUPLICATION

"You can say that again!"

Duplication has been recognized for more than 30 years as the bane of the programmer's lot. How does duplication cause problems?

- There is more code to maintain (a conceptual and physical burden).
- Parts that vary are buried inside the parts that stay the same (a perceptual problem—it's hard to see the important stuff).
- Code variations often hide deeper similarities—it will be hard to see the deeper solution among all the similar code.
- There's a tendency to fix a bug in one place and leave identical bugs elsewhere unfixed. When you see two variations of something, it's hard to know which variation is the right pattern or if there's a good reason for the variations.

David Parnas introduced the idea of information hiding: A good module has a secret. By ensuring that a module keeps its secret, we usually reduce duplication. (See "On the criteria to be used in decomposing systems into modules," *Communications of the ACM*, 15 [2], 1972.)

Duplication is a root problem. Many other smells are special-case indicators of duplication. Duplication is not always obvious, but it's critical that we address it. Strive to make your code express each idea "once and only once."

Smells Covered

- Magic Number
- Duplicated Code
- Alternative Classes with Different Interfaces

Magic Number

Symptoms

- A constant (other than the empty string; 0, 1, or perhaps 2; and a few other base cases) appears in the body of the code.

Causes

Someone needs a value, so they put it in the code. On its own, perhaps it's not so bad, but often there are other values derived from or dependent on it. For example, we'll have a string defined banana and a length variable of 6. If you change the string, you need to change the length variable; however, this is not obvious, and so a defect gets in.

This is often a simple form of duplication, and it's especially easy to spot.

What to Do

- *Replace Magic Number with Symbolic Constant* for the special value.
- If the values are strings (e.g., the text of dialog boxes), you may want to put them in some sort of mapping facility. (This is a move toward internationalization, and it often reduces duplication as well.)

Payoff

Reduces duplication. Improves communication.

Contraindications

Tests are often more readable when they simply use the value they want, but even in that case you might pull out a symbolic constant when there are derived values involved.

If you've moved to a map solution, the keys must be coordinated between the code and the map.

Duplicated Code

Symptoms

- *The easy form*: Two fragments of code look nearly identical.
- *The hard form*: Two fragments of code have nearly identical effects (at any conceptual level).

Causes

Some duplication occurs because programmers work independently in different parts of the system, and they don't realize that they are creating almost identical code. Sometimes people realize there's duplication, but they're too lazy to remove it. Other times, duplication will be hidden by other smells; once those smells are fixed, the duplication becomes more obvious.

A worse-case (but perhaps the most common) scenario occurs when the programmers intentionally duplicate code. They find some code that is *almost* right, so they copy and paste it into the new spot with some slight alterations.

What to Do

- If the duplication is within a method or in two different methods in the same class: Use *Extract Method* to pull the common part out into a separate method.
- If the duplication is within two sibling classes: Use *Extract Method* to create a single routine; then use *Pull Up Field* and/or *Pull Up Method* to bring the common parts together. Then you may be able to use *Form Template Method* to create a common algorithm in the parent and unique steps in the children.
- If the duplication is in two unrelated classes: Either extract the common part into a new class via *Extract Class*, or decide that the smell is *Feature Envy* (see Chapter 10) so the common code really belongs on only one class or the other.
- In any of these cases, you may find that the two places aren't literally identical but that they have the same

effect. Then you may do a *Substitute Algorithm* so that only one copy is involved.

Payoff

Reduces duplication. Lowers size. Can lead to better abstractions and more flexible code.

Contraindications

In very rare cases, you may conclude that the duplication communicates significantly better and decide to leave it in place. Or you may have duplication that is only coincidental; in this case, folding the two places together would only confuse the reader.

Alternative Classes with Different Interfaces

Symptoms

- Two classes seem to be doing the same thing but are using different method names.

Causes

People create similar code to handle a similar situation, but don't realize the other code exists.

What to Do

Harmonize classes so that you can eliminate one of them.

1. *Rename Method* to make method names similar.
2. *Move Method, Add Parameter,* and *Parameterize Method* to make protocols (method signatures and approach) similar.
3. If the two classes are similar but not identical, use *Extract Superclass* once you have them reasonably well harmonized.
4. Remove the extra class if possible.

Payoff

Reduces duplication. May also reduce size. May improve communication (by removing ambiguity about which approach to use).

Contraindications

Sometimes the two classes can't be changed (e.g., if both are in different libraries). Each library may have its own vision for the same concept, but you may be left with no good way to unify them.

Challenges

EXERCISE 13   Two Libraries. (Challenging).

You're trying to integrate two modules from two different sources. Each module has its own logging approach.

System A:

```
package com.fubar.log;
   public final class Log {
       public int INFO=1, WARN=2, ERROR=3, FATAL=4;
       public static void setLog(File f) {…}
       public static void log(int level, String msg) {…}
   }
```

Calls to `Log.log` are sprinkled throughout the code.

System B:

```
package com.bar.logger;
   public class Logger {
       public void informational(String msg) {…}
       public void informational(String msg, Exception e) {…}
       public void warning(String msg) {…}
       public void warning(String msg, Exception e) {…}
       public void fatal(String msg) {…}
       public void fatal(String msg, Exception e) {…}
   }

   public class LogFacility {
       public Logger makeLogger(String id) {…}
       public static void setOutput(OutputStream out) {…}
   }
```

Objects that may need to log hold a Logger object.

Your long-term goal is to move to the new standard logging facility in JDK 1.4, but your environment doesn't support that yet.

EXERCISE 13   Two Libraries. (Challenging). (Continued)

> A. **What overall approach would you use to harmonize these classes with where you want to go? (Make sure to address the JDK 1.4 concern.)**
>
> B. **Create a simple test for each logger, and implement the logger with the simplest approach possible.**
>
> C. **Harmonize the classes so you can eliminate one of them. (Don't worry about the JDK 1.4 future yet.)**
>
> ■ *See Appendix A for solutions.*

EXERCISE 14   Properties.

(Online at *www.xp123.com/rwb*)

```java
public void getTimes(Properties props)
throws Exception {
  String valueString;
  int value;

  valueString = props.getProperty("interval");
  if (valueString == null) {
    throw new MissingPropertiesException("monitor interval");
  }
  value = Integer.parseInt(valueString);

  if (value <= 0) {
    throw new MissingPropertiesException("monitor interval > 0");
  }
  checkInterval = value;

  valueString = props.getProperty("duration");
  if (valueString == null) {
    throw new MissingPropertiesException("duration");
  }
```

EXERCISE 14   Properties. (Continued)

```
  value = Integer.parseInt(valueString);
  if (value <= 0) {
    throw new MissingPropertiesException("duration > 0");
  }
  if ((value % checkInterval) != 0) {
    throw new MissingPropertiesException("duration % checkInterval");
  }
  monitorTime = value;

  valueString = props.getProperty("departure");
  if (valueString == null) {
    throw new MissingPropertiesException("departure offset");
  }
  value = Integer.parseInt(valueString);
  if (value <= 0) {
    throw new MissingPropertiesException("departure > 0");
  }
  if ((value % checkInterval) != 0) {
    throw new MissingPropertiesException("departure % checkInterval");
  }
  departureOffset = value;
}
```

   A. How would you handle the duplication? Notice that determination of the
   checkInterval **doesn't involve %.**

   ■ *See Appendix A for solutions.*

EXERCISE 15   Template Example.

(originally in *Extreme Programming Explored*). (Online at *www.xp123.com/rwb*)

```
try {    String template = new String(sourceTemplate);
    // Substitute for %CODE%
    int templateSplitBegin = template.indexOf("%CODE%");
    int templateSplitEnd = templateSplitBegin + 6;
    String templatePartOne = new String(
        template.substring(0, templateSplitBegin));
    String templatePartTwo = new String(
        template.substring(templateSplitEnd, template.length()));
    code = new String(reqId);
    template = new String(templatePartOne + code + templatePartTwo);
```

EXERCISE 15   Template Example. (Continued)

```
    // Substitute for %ALTCODE%
    templateSplitBegin = template.indexOf("%ALTCODE%");
    templateSplitEnd = templateSplitBegin + 9;
    templatePartOne = new String(
        template.substring(0, templateSplitBegin));
    templatePartTwo = new String(
        template.substring(templateSplitEnd, template.length()));
    altcode = code.substring(0,5) + "-" + code.substring(5,8);
    out.print(templatePartOne + altcode + templatePartTwo);
} catch (Exception e) {
    System.out.println("Error in substitute()");
}
```

A. What duplication do you see?

B. What would you do to remove the duplication?

C. One piece that repeats is a structure of the form `new String(`**some other string**`)`**.
What does this code do? What does this have to do with the** `intern()` **method on class
String? Does it apply here?**

◼ *See Appendix A for solutions.*

EXERCISE 16   Duplicate Observed Data. (Challenging).

The refactoring *Duplicate Observed Data* works like this:

**If you have domain data in a widget-type class, move the domain data to a new domain
class, and set up an observer so that the widget is notified of any changes to it.**

**Thus, we've taken a situation where data was in one place, and we have not only duplicated
it, but we've also added a need for synchronization between two objects.**

EXERCISE 16 Duplicate Observed Data. (Challenging). (Continued)

>   **A. Why is this duplication considered acceptable (desirable, even)? (Hint: Your answer should touch on the Observer or Model-View-Controller pattern.)**
>
>   **B. What are the performance implications of this approach?**
>
>   ■ *See Appendix A for solutions.*

EXERCISE 17 Java Libraries.

>   **A. The Java libraries have several places where there is duplication. Describe some examples of this. They might be at a low, medium, or high level.**
>
>   **B. Why does this duplication exist? Is it worth it?**
>
>   ■ *See Appendix A for solutions.*

EXERCISE 18 Points.

Suppose you see these two classes:

```
public class Bird {
   // ...
   public void move(Point vector) {
      x += vector.x % maxX;
      y += vector.y % maxY;
   }
}

public class Button {
   // ...
   public void setPosition(Point p) {
      x = p.x;
      while (x >= maxX) x -= maxX;
      while (x < 0) x += maxX;
```

EXERCISE 18   Points. (Continued)

```
        y = p.y;
        while (y >= maxY) y -= maxY;
        while (y < 0) y += maxY;
    }

}
```

A. What is the duplication?

B. What could you do to eliminate duplication in these two classes?

C. Sometimes, two versions of duplicated code are similar, but one has fixed a bug and the other hasn't. How can refactoring help you in this situation?

■ *See Appendix A for solutions.*

EXERCISE 19   Expression.

Suppose we have an expression that is structured in tree form. So the tree for 3 + 4 ∗ 5 might look like this:

```
    +
   / \
  3   *
     / \
    4   5
```

EXERCISE 19   Expression. (Continued)

The class hierarchy might look like this:

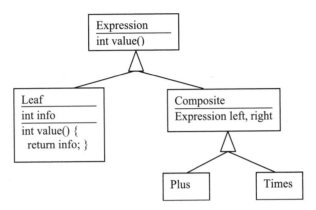

The code for Plus.value():

```
public int value() {
   int v1 = left.value();
   int v2 = right.value();
   return v1 + v2;
}
```

The code for Times.value():

```
public int value() {
   int v1 = left.value();
   int v2 = right.value();
   return v1 * v2;
}
```

A. What steps would you take to reduce the duplication?

■ *See Appendix A for solutions.*

7

CONDITIONAL LOGIC

"If wishes were horses, beggars would ride."

It's natural that object-oriented programming is focused on objects and their relationships, but the code within an object is important too. Classic books like Jon Bentley's *Programming Pearls* or Brian Kernighan and P. J. Pike's *Elements of Programming Style* can help inspire you to write good, clean code.

Conditional logic is often the trickiest part of such code.

- It's hard to reason about, since we have to consider multiple paths through the code.
- It's tempting to add special-case handling rather than develop the general case.
- Conditional logic sometimes is used as a weak substitute for object-oriented mechanisms.

Smells Covered

- Null Check
- Complicated Boolean Expression
- Special Case
- Simulated Inheritance (Switch Statement)

Null Check

Symptoms

- There are repeated occurrences of code like this:
  ```
  if (xxx == null) …
  ```

Causes

Someone decides, "We'll use null to mean the default." This may let them avoid the trouble of initializing certain fields or of creating certain objects, or it may be an afterthought for an unexpected case. The null check may be introduced to work around a null-pointer bug (without addressing the underlying cause).

What to Do

- If there's a reasonable default value, use that.
- Otherwise, *Introduce Null Object* to create a default object that you explicitly use.

Payoff

Reduces duplication. Reduces logic errors and exceptions.

Contraindications

- If the null check occurs in only one place (e.g., in a factory method), it is usually not worth the effort to create a separate Null Object.
- Null objects need to have safe behavior for the methods they provide. They often act like *identity* objects (as 0 does relative to addition). If you can't define a safe behavior for each method, you may not be able to use a Null Object.
- Watch out for a case where null means two or more different things in different contexts. (You may be able to support this with different Null Objects.)

EXERCISE 20   Null Object.

> Consider the code in Exercise 4 (Chapter 3).
>
> A. Some of the null checks are checks for null strings. One alternate approach would be to use empty strings. What are the downsides of this approach (taking into account the test and all the other client classes you don't see here)?

EXERCISE 20   Null Object. (Continued)

B. What's another approach to this problem?

C. Extract a Bin class, and introduce a Null object.

■ *See Appendix A for solutions.*

Complicated Boolean Expression

Symptoms

- Code has complex conditions involving and, or, and not.

Causes

The code may have been complicated from the beginning, or it may have picked up additional conditions along the way.

What to Do

- Apply DeMorgan's Law:
    ```
    ! (a && b)  => (!a) || (!b)
    ```

    and

    ```
    !(a || b)  =>  (!a) && (!b)
    ```

You may find that some variables will communicate better if they change names to reflect their flipped sense.

- *Introduce Explaining Variable* to make each clause clearer.
- Use guard clauses to *peel off* certain conditions; the remaining clauses get simpler.
- *Decompose Conditional* to pull each part into its own method.

Payoff

Improves communication.

Contraindications

You may be able to find other ways to simplify the expressions, or you may find that the rewritten expression communicates less well.

EXERCISE 21   Conditional Expression.

Consider this code fragment:

```
if (!((score > 700) ||
    ((income >= 40000) && (income <= 100000)
   && authorized && (score > 500)) ||
    (income > 100000)))
    reject();
else
    accept();
```

A. Apply DeMorgan's Law to simplify this as much as possible.

B. Starting from the original, rewrite the condition by introducing explaining variables.

C. Starting from the original, flip the `if` and `else` clauses, then break the original into several `if` clauses. (You'll call `accept()` in three different places.)

D. Consolidate Conditional Expression by extracting a method to compute the condition.

E. Which approach was the simplest? The clearest? Can you combine the techniques?

EXERCISE 21 Conditional Expression. (Continued)

> F. **Describe the conditions in tabular form. Base the rows and columns on three variables: one for the three score ranges, one for the income ranges, and one for the authorized flag. The cells in the table should say either "accept" or "reject."**
>
> ■ *See Appendix A for solutions.*

Special Case

Symptoms

- Complex `if` statements
- Checks for particular values before doing work (especially comparisons to constants or enumerations)

Causes

Someone realizes a special case is needed.

What to Do

- If the conditionals are taking the place of polymorphism, *Replace Conditional with Polymorphism*.
- If the `if` and `then` clauses are similar enough, you may be able to rewrite them so that the same code fragment can generate the proper results for each case; then the conditional can be eliminated.

Payoff

Improves communication. May expose duplication.

Contraindications

- In a recursive definition, there is always a base case that will stop the recursion; you can't expect to eliminate these.
- Sometimes an `if` clause is just the simplest way to do something.

Simulated Inheritance (Switch Statement)

Symptoms

- Code uses a switch statement (especially on a type field).
- Code has several if statements in a row (especially if they're comparing against the same value).
- Code uses instanceof (or its equivalent) to decide what type it's working with.

Causes

This smell is often caused by laziness in introducing new classes. The first time you need conditional behavior, you might use an if or switch statement rather than a new class. It's not a big problem at this point because it occurs only once. Then say you need another condition based on the same type code, and you introduce a second switch instead of fixing the lack of polymorphism.

Sometimes the lack of polymorphism is hidden behind a series of if statements instead of an explicit switch statement, but the root problem is the same.

What to Do

Don't simulate inheritance—use mechanisms built into the programming language.

- If a switch statement on the same condition occurs in several places, it is often using a *type code*; replace this with the polymorphism built into objects. It takes a series of refactorings to make this change:

  1. *Extract Method*. Pull out the code for each branch.
  2. *Move Method*. Move related code onto the right class.
  3. *Replace Type Code with Subclass* or *Replace Type Code with State/Strategy*. Set up the inheritance structure.
  4. *Replace Conditional with Polymorphism*. Eliminate the conditionals.

- If the conditions occur within a single class, you might be able to replace the conditional logic via *Replace Parameter with Explicit Methods* or *Introduce Null Object*.

Payoff

Improves communication. May expose duplication.

Contraindications

Sometimes a switch statement is the simplest way to express the logic. If the code is doing something simple, in one place, you may not feel the need for a separate class. This may be especially common for places that are interfacing with non-object-oriented parts of the system. Michael Feathers says, "I'm okay with switches if they convert data into objects."

A single switch statement is sometimes used in a Factory or Abstract Factory (for more information, see Gamma's *Design Patterns*). This one place decides how to configure the whole factory. You can sometimes replace it with Class.forName() (i.e., dynamic class loading), but that is not always attractive for security, communication, or performance reasons.

Sometimes a switch statement is used in several related places to control a state machine. Decide whether it makes more sense as is, or whether the State pattern (see Gamma's *Design Patterns*) is more appropriate.

EXERCISE 22   Switch Statement.

> **Consider this code:**
>
> ```
> public void printIt(Operation op) {
>     String out = "?";
>     switch (op.type) {
>     case '+': out = "push"; break;
>     case '-': out = "pop"; break;
>     case '@': out = "top"; break;
>     default: out = "unknown";
>     }
>     System.out.println("operation=" + out);
> }
>
> public void doIt(Operation op, Stack s, Object item) {
>     switch (op.type) {
>     case '+': s.push(item); break;
>     case '-': s.pop(); break;
>     }
> }
> ```
>
> **A. What would you do?**
>
> ■ *See Appendix A for solutions.*

EXERCISE 23   Factory Method. (Challenging).

Consider this class structure:

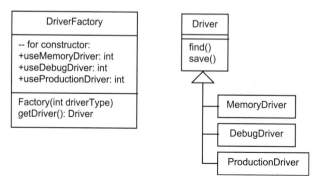

A. **Write code for the factory according to the implied design. Note: One of the three constants is passed to the constructor; this determines what type driver will be returned by** getDriver().

B. **Your code probably smells of a** switch **statement (even if it's implemented using** if**). Is this conditional logic justified?**

C. **Some factories use dynamic class loading—via** Class.forName()**—to load the correct class on demand. Modify your factory to accept a string argument (the name of the driver class) and load the instance dynamically.**
Your code no longer mentions the types explicitly. What are some advantages to that? (Hint: Think of the impact on building the system.)

D. **What are some disadvantages to this new arrangement?**

■ *See Appendix A for solutions.*

INTERLUDE 3 DESIGN PATTERNS

INTERLUDE I3.1 Patterns.

Following is a list of design patterns described in Gamma's *Design Patterns.* What refactorings might you use to evolve to some of these patterns?

Creational patterns

    ___ Abstract Factory

    ___ Builder

    ___ Factory Method

    ___ Prototype

    ___ Singleton

Structural Patterns

    ___ Adapter

    ___ Bridge

    ___ Composite

    ___ Decorator

    ___ Façade

    ___ Flyweight

    ___ Proxy

INTERLUDE I3.1   Patterns. (Continued)

Behavioral Patterns

___ Chain of Responsibility

___ Command

___ Interpreter

___ Iterator

___ Mediator

___ Memento

___ Observer

___ State

___ Strategy

___ Template Method

___ Visitor

■ *See Appendix A for solutions.*

SECTION 2

SMELLS BETWEEN CLASSES

8

DATA

Data can be defined as simple facts, divorced from information about what to do with them. "Data" has a dusty whiff about it, the old-fashioned ring of *data processing* or *data structures*.

Data is often a natural starting point for thinking about things. For example, we know we have a first name, middle name, and last name, so we create a Person class with that information. But *objects* are about *data* and *behavior* together—your code will be more robust if you organize objects by behavior.

Data-oriented objects are an opportunity. The smells in this chapter are often signs of a missing or inadequately formed class. If the data represents a good clustering, we'll usually be able to find behavior that belongs in the class.

Smells Covered

- Primitive Obsession
- Data Class
- Data Clump
- Temporary Field

Primitive Obsession

Symptoms

Look for:

- Uses of the primitive or near-primitive types (int, float, String, etc.)
- Constants and enumerations representing small integers
- String constants representing field names

Causes

Several things can cause overuse of primitives:

- *Missing class:* Since almost all data must be in a primitive somewhere, it's easy to start with a primitive and miss an opportunity to introduce a new class.
- *Simulated types:* Some primitives act as type codes, in effect, simulating objects. A class may start with one behavior, then pick up a boolean to say which of two behaviors are used, and then there may be an enumeration of small values to say which of several behaviors to use. But by then, it may well be hiding a need for multiple classes.
- *Simulated field accessors:* Sometimes a primitive is used as an index to provide access to pseudofields in an array. Strings are occasionally used this way with HashTables or Maps.

What to Do

For **missing objects**:

- See Data Clump (this chapter), because the primitives can often be encapsulated by addressing that problem.
- *Replace Data Value with Object* to make first-class data values.

For **simulated types**, an integer type code stands in for a class.

- If no behavior is conditional on the type code, then it is more like an enumeration, so *Replace Type Code with Class.*
- If the type code is immutable and the class is not subclassed already, *Replace Type Code with Subclass.*
- If the type code changes or the class is subclassed already, *Replace Type Code with State/Strategy.* In Fowler's *Refactoring,* there's an example of this transformation in the description of *Replace Conditional with Polymorphism.*

For **simulated field accessors**:

- If the primitive is used to treat certain array elements specially, *Replace Array with Object.*

Payoff

Improves communication. May expose duplication. Improves flexibility. Often exposes the need for other refactorings.

Contraindications

- Primitives that are really missing objects are so common that I hesitate to provide any excuses for not introducing the object. There are occasionally dependency or performance issues that stop you from addressing this smell.
- A Map can sometimes be used instead of an object with fixed fields, by using the names of fields as indices. This can reduce coupling to the structure of a simple object, but at some cost in performance, type safety, and clarity.

Notes

- A close relative of this problem occurs when ArrayList (or some other generic structure) is overused.

EXERCISE 24 Alternative Representations.

Suggest two or three alternative representations for each of these types.

Money:

Position (in a list):

Range:

Social Security Number (government identification number: "123-45-6789"):

Telephone number:

Street Address ("123 E. Main Street"):

ZIP (postal) code:

■ *See Appendix A for solutions.*

EXERCISE 25   A Counterargument.

Consider a business application in which a user enters a ZIP code (among other things) and it gets stored in a relational database. Someone argues: "It's not worth the bother of turning it into an object; when it gets written, it will just have to be turned into a primitive again." Why might it be worth creating the object in spite of the need for two conversions?

■ *See Appendix A for solutions.*

EXERCISE 26   Iterator.

How does an Iterator or Enumerator reduce primitive obsession?

■ *See Appendix A for solutions.*

EXERCISE 27   Editor.

Consider this interface to an editor:

```
public class Editor {
    public void insert(String text) {…}
    public String fetch(int numberOfCharactersToFetch) {…}
    public void moveTo(int position) {…}
    public int position() {…}
    // more, omitted
}
```

and this sequence of calls:

```
editor.insert("ba(nana)");
int firstParendPosition = 2;
editor.moveTo(firstParendPosition);
assertEquals("(", editor.fetch(1));

editor.moveTo(1);
editor.insert("x");    // Now: bxa(nana)
editor.moveTo(firstParendPosition);
assertEquals(___, editor.fetch(1));
```

A. Given the interface provided, what string would you expect to use in place of the ___?

B. **Based on the variable name** (`firstParendPosition`), **what string might you like to use instead? Of what use would this be?**

C. **The crux of the problem is the use of** `int` **as a position index. Suggest an alternative approach.**

D. **Relate your solution to the Memento design pattern (from Gamma's *Design Patterns*).**

■ *See Appendix A for solutions.*

Data Class

Symptoms

- The class consists only of public data members, or of simple getting and setting methods. This lets clients depend on the mutability and representation of the class.

Causes

It's common for classes to begin like this: You realize that some data is part of an independent object, so you extract it. But objects are about the commonality of *behavior*, and these objects aren't developed enough as yet to have much behavior.

What to Do

1. *Encapsulate Field* to block direct access to the fields (allowing access only through getters and setters).
2. *Remove Setting Methods* for any methods you can.
3. *Encapsulate Collection* to remove direct access to any collection-type fields.
4. Look at each client of the object. Almost invariably, you'll find clients accessing the fields and manipulating the results when the class could do it for them. (This is

often a source of duplication, because many callers will tend to do the same things with the data.) Use *Extract Method* on the client to pull out the class-related code, then *Move Method* to put it over on the class.

5. After doing this awhile, you may find that you have several similar methods on the class. Use refactorings such as *Rename Method, Extract Method, Add Parameter,* or *Remove Parameter* to harmonize signatures and remove duplication.

6. Most access to the fields shouldn't be needed anymore because the moved methods cover the real use. So use *Hide Method* to eliminate access to the getters and setters. (You may decide to keep them with private access and have all internal access go through them.)

Payoff

Improves communication. May expose duplication (as you'll often find clients manipulating the fields in similar ways).

Contraindications

There are times when the encapsulation of fields can have a performance cost. For example, consider a point with *x* and *y* coordinates. The interface (probably) isn't going to change, and people may deal with *lots* of points. So, in Java, the Point class makes its fields public. (This saves the cost of a procedure call for each access.)

Some persistence mechanisms rely on reflection or getter/setter methods to see fields to determine what data should be loaded or stored. For these classes, you may never be able to eliminate their data class nature. If I'm stuck with this, I try to treat these classes as Mementos (see Gamma's *Design Patterns*). Sometimes I'll use another class as a layer above these persistence-only classes; that new class can benefit from all the changes described above, and it will hide the low-level classes.

EXERCISE 28   Library Classes.

> **Compare these library classes. What do they have in common?**

```
java.awt.Event
java.awt.GridBagConstraints
java.awt.Insets
```

EXERCISE 28 Library Classes. (Continued)

```
java.awt.Point
java.awt.Polygon
java.awt.Rectangle
```

■ *See Appendix A for solutions.*

EXERCISE 29 Color and Date.

The classes java.awt.Color and java.util.Date are examples of classes encapsulated such that access to members is only through methods.

A. Propose at least two internal representations for each class.

B. How does having no direct access to members promote the ability of a class to be immutable?

■ *See Appendix A for solutions.*

EXERCISE 30 Proper Names. (Challenging).

A. Clean up this Data Class. (Online at *www.xp123.com/rwb*)

Person.java

```java
public class Person {
    public String last;
    public String first;
    public String middle;

    public Person(String last, String first, String middle) {
        this.last = last;
        this.first = first;
        this.middle = middle;
    }
}
```

EXERCISE 30   Proper Names. (Challenging). (Continued)

PersonClient.java

```java
// The clients are in one file for convenience;
// imagine them as non-test methods in separate client classes.

import junit.framework.TestCase;

import java.io.*

public class PersonClient extends TestCase {
    public PersonClient(String name) {super(name);}

    public void client1(Writer out, Person person) throws IOException {
        out.write(person.first);
        out.write(" ");
        if (person.middle != null) {
            out.write(person.middle);
            out.write(" ");
        }
        out.write(person.last);
    }

    public String client2(Person person) {
        String result = person.last + ", " + person.first;
        if (person.middle != null)
            result += " " + person.middle;
        return result;
    }

    public void client3(Writer out, Person person) throws IOException {
        out.write(person.last);
        out.write(", ");
        out.write(person.first);
        if (person.middle != null) {
            out.write(" ");
            out.write(person.middle);
        }
    }

    public String client4(Person person) {
        return person.last + ", " +
                person.first +
                ((person.middle == null) ? "" : " " + person.middle);
    }
```

EXERCISE 30 Proper Names. (Challenging). (Continued)

```
public void testClients() throws IOException {
    Person bobSmith = new Person("Smith", "Bob", null);
    Person jennyJJones = new Person("Jones", "Jenny", "J");
    StringWriter out = new StringWriter();
    client1(out, bobSmith);
    assertEquals("Bob Smith", out.toString());

    out = new StringWriter();
    client1(out, jennyJJones);
    assertEquals("Jenny J Jones", out.toString());

    assertEquals("Smith, Bob", client2(bobSmith));
    assertEquals("Jones, Jenny J", client2(jennyJJones));

    out = new StringWriter();
    client3(out, bobSmith);
    assertEquals("Smith, Bob", out.toString());

    out = new StringWriter();
    client3(out, jennyJJones);
    assertEquals("Jones, Jenny J", out.toString());

    assertEquals("Smith, Bob", client4(bobSmith));
    assertEquals("Jones, Jenny J", client4(jennyJJones));
    }
}
```

   B. There's a new requirement to support people with only one name (say, Cher or
   Madonna) or with several last names (Oscar de los Santos). Compare the difficulty of
   this change before and after your refactoring in the previous part.

Data Clump

Symptoms

- The same two or three items frequently appear together
  in classes and parameter lists.
- The code declares some fields, then methods that work
  with those fields, then more fields and more methods,
  etc. (i.e., there are groups of fields and methods together
  within the class).
- Groups of field names start or end with similar substrings.

Causes

The items are typically part of some other entity, but as yet no one has had the insight to realize that there's a missing class. Or sometimes, people know the class is missing, but think it's too small or unimportant to stand alone.

(Identifying these classes is often a major step toward simplifying a system, and it often helps you to generalize classes more easily.)

What to Do

- If the items are fields in a class, use *Extract Class* to pull them into a new class.
- If the values are together in method signatures, *Introduce Parameter Object* to extract the new object.
- Look at calls that pass around the items from the new object to see if they can *Preserve Whole Object* instead.
- Look at uses of the items; there are often opportunities to use *Move Method*, etc., to move those uses into the new object (as you would to address the Data Class smell).

Payoff

Improves communication. May expose duplication. Usually reduces size.

Contraindications

Occasionally, passing a whole object will introduce a dependency you don't want (as lower-level classes get exposed to the whole new object instead of just its values). So you may pass in the pieces to prevent this dependency.

Very rarely, there is a measured performance problem solved by passing in the parts of the object instead of the object itself. Recognize that this is a compromise in the object model for performance. Such code is worth commenting!

Temporary Field

Symptoms

- A field is set only at certain times, and it is null (or unused) at other times.

Causes

This can happen when one part of an object has an algorithm that passes around information through the fields rather than through parameters; the fields are valid or used only when the algorithm is active. That the fields are sometimes used and sometimes not suggests that there may be a missing object whose life cycle differs from that of the object holding it.

What to Do

- *Extract Class*, moving over the fields and any related code.

Payoff

Improves communication and clarity. May reduce duplication, especially if other places can make use of the new class.

Contraindications

It may not be worth the trouble of creating a new object if it doesn't represent a useful abstraction.

9

INHERITANCE

The relationship between a class and its subclass often starts being simple but gets more complicated over time. A subclass will often depend on its parent more intimately than will a separate class, but it can go too far.

A key challenge is deciding what a class *is* versus what a class *has*. A class structure often starts with inheritance and moves to a more compositional style over time.

Smells Covered

- Refused Bequest
- Inappropriate Intimacy (Subclass Form)
- Lazy Class

See also these other smells related to inheritance:

- Simulated Inheritance (Switch Statement), Chapter 7
- Parallel Inheritance Hierarchies, Chapter 11
- Combinatorial Explosion, Chapter 11

Refused Bequest

Symptoms

- A class inherits from a parent, but throws an exception instead of supporting a method (honest refusal).
- A class inherits from a parent, but an inherited method just doesn't work when called on the class (implicit refusal).
- Clients tend to access the class through a handle to the subclass rather than through a handle to the parent.

- Inheritance doesn't really make sense; the subclass just isn't an example of the parent.

Causes

A class may inherit from another class just for implementation convenience without really intending the class to be substitutable for the parent. Or, there may be a conscious decision to let subclasses deny use of some features to prevent an explosion of types for all feature combinations.

What to Do

- If it's not confusing, you might decide to leave it as is.
- If there's no reason to share a class relationship, then *Replace Inheritance with Delegation*.
- If the parent-child relationship *does* make sense, you can create a new child class via *Extract Subclass, Push Down Field*, and *Push Down Method*. See Figure 9.1. Let this class hold the nonrefused behavior, and change clients of the parent to be clients of the new class—then the parent need not mention the feature. You may be able to eliminate the refused methods from the original class and the parent.

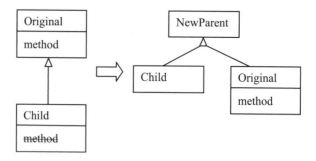

FIGURE 9.1 Rearranging the hierarchy.

Payoff

Improves communication. Improves testability (because you don't have to worry about different capabilities up and down the class hierarchy).

Contraindications

Sometimes a Refused Bequest is used to prevent an explosion of new types. (By refusing specific methods, we don't need to create a hierarchy of types for the various combinations of refusals.)

Notes

There is a guideline known as the Liskov Substitution Principle (LSP). It says that you should be able to treat any subclass of a class as an example of that class. Rejecting a parent's method violates this guideline. The Eiffel language embodies that principle in its use of preconditions and postconditions: A method can require less, but it must promise at least as much as its parent. See Robert Martin's book, *Agile Software Development: Principles, Patterns, and Practices*, for a broader explanation of the LSP.

EXERCISE 31   Collection Classes.

The Collection classes in Java don't have a separate hierarchy for read-only collections; they just provide a "wrapper" that will refuse to make changes to its underlying collection.

  A. Which approach to spotting this applies here?

  B. Explain why a class that uses a read-only collection doesn't have to catch or declare an exception.

  C. Do you agree with the library designers' approach? What other approach could they have used?

■ *See Appendix A for solutions.*

EXERCISE 32   Refused Bequest.

> **Find an example of a Refused Bequest in code that you have access to.**

Inappropriate Intimacy (Subclass Form)

Symptoms

- A class accesses internal (should-be-private) parts of its parent. (There is a related form of Inappropriate Intimacy between separate classes; see "Inappropriate Intimacy [General Form]," Chapter 10.)

Causes

It's natural that parent and child classes be more coupled together than two strangers. Sometimes this just goes too far.

What to Do

- If the subclass is accessing the parent's fields in an uncontrolled way, use *Self Encapsulate Field*.
- If the parent can define a general algorithm that the children can plug into, then use *Form Template Method*.
- If the parent and child need to be even more decoupled, then *Replace Inheritance with Delegation*.

Payoff

Reduces duplication. Often improves communication. May reduce size.

Contraindications

None identified.

Lazy Class

Symptoms

- A class isn't doing much—its parents, children, or callers seem to be doing all the associated work, and there isn't enough behavior left in the class to justify its continued existence.

Causes

Typically, all the class's responsibilities have been moved to other places in the course of refactoring.

What to Do

- If parents or children of the class seem like the right place for the class's behavior, fold it into one of them via *Collapse Hierarchy.*
- Otherwise, fold its behavior into its caller via *Inline Class.*

Payoff

Reduces size. Improves communication. Improves simplicity.

Contraindications

- Sometimes a lazy class is present to communicate intent. You may have to balance communication versus simplicity.

EXERCISE 33   Swing Libraries. (Challenging),

The Swing Libraries have a pattern:

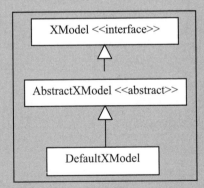

The AbstractXModel is the only implementation of the interface, and the DefaultXModel is the only subclass of the AbstractXModel. (Typically the abstract model has the notification handling built in, but it may support other things.)

EXERCISE 33   Swing Libraries. (Challenging), (Continued)

A. What advantages are there in having the model be an interface, separate from the AbstractXModel class?

B. Why is this not an example of a Lazy Class?

C. Should you adopt this three-class structure for your object structure?

■ *See Appendix A for solutions.*

10

RESPONSIBILITY

It's hard to get the right balance of responsibility between objects. One of the beauties of refactoring is that it lets us experiment with different ideas in a way that safely lets us change our minds.

There are tools we can use to help us decide how our objects should work together, namely, design patterns and CRC cards (see *www.c2.com/cgi/wiki?CrcCards*).

Refactorings are often reversible, and they may trade off between two good things. A nice example of this is Message Chains versus Middle Man. Sometimes there's a way to improve both smells at the same time, but many times it's a balancing act between them.

Smells Covered

- Feature Envy
- Inappropriate Intimacy (General Form)
- Message Chains
- Middle Man

Feature Envy

Symptoms

- A method seems to be focused on manipulating the data of other classes rather than its own. (You may notice this because of duplication—several clients do the same manipulation, or you may see the same object touched several times in a row.)

Causes

This is very common among clients of current and former data classes, but you can see it for any class and its clients.

What to Do

- *Move Method* to put the actions on the correct class. (You may have to *Extract Method* first to isolate the misplaced part.)

Payoff

Reduces duplication. Often improves communication (since code moves to where people would expect it to be). May expose further refactoring opportunities.

Contraindications

Sometimes behavior is intentionally put on the "wrong" class. For example, some design patterns, such as Strategy or Visitor, pull behavior to a separate class so it can be independently changed. If you *Move Method* to put it back, you can end up putting things together that should change separately.

Notes

It's not always easy to distinguish Feature Envy from Inappropriate Intimacy (later in this chapter). Joshua Kerievsky of Industrial Logic suggests, "Feature Envy is when a class does so little on its own that it needs to ask lots of other classes things in order to do anything on its own. Inappropriate Intimacy is when a class reaches deep inside another class to get access to stuff it shouldn't have access to."

EXERCISE 34 Feature Envy.

> Look back at Exercise 4 (Chapter 3). In `Report.report()`, notice how the information being printed is obtained by looking inside a Machine or Robot's fields. Fix these two examples of Feature Envy.

■ *See Appendix A for solutions.*

Inappropriate Intimacy (General Form)

Symptoms

- One class accesses internal (should-be-private) parts of another class. (There is a related form of Inappropriate Intimacy between a subclass and its parents; see "Inappropriate Intimacy [Subclass Form]," Chapter 9.)

Causes

The two classes probably became intertwined a little at a time. By the time you realize there's a problem, they're coupled. There may be a missing class that should mediate between them. This problem is more serious between unrelated classes than between a parent and child.

What to Do

- If two independent classes are entangled, use *Move Method* and *Move Field* to put the right pieces on the right class.
- If the tangled part seems to be a missing class, use *Extract Class* and *Hide Delegate* to introduce the new class.
- If classes point to each other, use *Change Bidirectional Reference to Unidirectional* to turn it into a one-way dependency.
- If a subclass is too coupled to its parent (as explained in "Inappropriate Intimacy [Subclass Form]," Chapter 9)
  - If the subclass is accessing the parent's fields in an uncontrolled way, use *Self Encapsulate Field*.
  - If the parent can define a general algorithm that the children can plug into, then use *Form Template Method*.
  - If the parent and child need to be even more decoupled, then *Replace Inheritance with Delegation*.

Payoff

Reduces duplication. Often improves communication. May reduce size.

Contraindications

None identified.

Message Chains

Symptoms

- You see calls of the form:
  a.b().c().d()
  (This may happen directly or through intermediate results.)

Causes

An object must cooperate with other objects to get things done, and that is OK; the problem is that this couples both the objects *and* the path to get to them. This sort of coupling goes against two maxims of object-oriented programming: *Tell, Don't Ask* and the *Law of Demeter*. Tell, Don't Ask says that, instead of *asking* for objects so that you can manipulate them, you simply *tell* them to do the manipulation for you. It's phrased even more clearly in the Law of Demeter: A method shouldn't talk to strangers; that is, it should talk only to itself, its arguments, its own fields, or the objects it creates. (Andrew Hunt and David Thomas's *The Pragmatic Programmer* describes both of these rules in more detail.)

What to Do

- If the manipulations actually belong on the target object (the one at the end of the chain), use *Extract Method* and *Move Method* to put them there.
- Use *Hide Delegate* to make the method depend on one object only. (So, rather than a.b().c().d(), put a d() method on the a object. That may require adding a d() method to the b() and c() objects as well.)

Payoff

May reduce or expose duplication.

Contraindications

This is a trade-off refactoring. If you apply *Hide Delegate* too much, you get to the point where everything's so busy delegating that nothing seems to be doing any actual work. Sometimes, it's just easier and less confusing to call a small chain.

Middle Man

Symptoms

- Most methods of a class call the same or a similar method on another object:

      f() {delegate.f();}

  (A class that mostly delegates its work is known as a *middle man*.)

Causes

For one thing, this can result from applying *Hide Delegate* to address Message Chains. Perhaps other features have moved out since then, and you're left with mostly delegating methods.

What to Do

- In general, *Remove Middle Man* by having the client call the delegate directly.
- If the delegate is owned by the middle man or is immutable, and the middle man has behavior to add, and the middle man can be seen as an example of the delegate, you might *Replace Delegation with Inheritance*.

Payoff

Reduces size. May improve communication.

Contraindications

- Some patterns (e.g., Proxy or Decorator) intentionally create delegates. Don't remove a Middle Man that's there for a reason.
- Middle Man and Message Chain trade off against each other.
- Delegates provide a sort of façade, letting a caller remain unaware of details of messages and structures. Removing a Middle Man can expose clients to more information than they should know.

Challenges

EXERCISE 35   Walking a List.

Consider the code used in Exercise 4 (Chapter 3).

A. How is walking the list of machines a case of Feature Envy or Inappropriate Intimacy?

B. Address this by extracting a new class. Make sure it has a report() method.

EXERCISE 36   Middle Man. (Challenging).

Consider these classes:

(This code has been greatly simplified; the queue wasn't originally storing strings.)

Queue.java

```
import java.util.ArrayList;

public class Queue {
    ArrayList delegate = new ArrayList();
    public Queue() {}
    public void addRear(String s) {delegate.add(s);}
    public int getSize() {return delegate.size();}

    public String removeFront() {
        String result = delegate.get(0).toString();
        delegate.remove(0);
        return result;
    }
}
```

QueueTest.java (selection)

```
public void testQ() {
  Queue q = new Queue();
  q.addRear("E1");
  q.addRear("E2");
```

EXERCISE 36 Middle Man. (Challenging). (Continued)

```
        assertEquals("E1", q.removeFront());
        assertEquals("E2", q.removeFront());
        assertEquals(0, q.getSize());
}
```

A. *Remove Middle Man* so that the queue is no longer a middle man for the ArrayList. Is this an improvement?

B. Put the Middle Man back in via *Hide Delegate*.

■ *See Appendix A for solutions.*

EXERCISE 37 Cart. (Challenging).

Consider these classes:

Here is Cart.cost():

```
public int cost() {
    int total = 0;
    for (int i=0; i < purchases.size(); i++) {
        Purchase p = (Purchase) purchases.elementAt(i);
        total += p.item().cost + p.shipping().cost;
    }
    return total;
}
```

EXERCISE 37   Cart. (Challenging). (Continued)

   A. Write the implied classes (and tests). The maxDays() method computes the largest number of days for any ShippingOption in the purchase.

   B. Apply *Hide Delegate* so Cart accesses only Purchase directly.

   C. *Hide Delegate* causes the Middle Man (Purchase) class to have a wider interface; that is, it exposes more methods. But applying that refactoring can open up a way to make the interface narrower. Explain this apparent contradiction.

   D. Use this line of reasoning to narrow the Purchase interface.

   E. Notice that the primitive int type is used to represent money. Would it be easier to introduce a Money class before or after the delegate changes?

   ■ *See Appendix A for solutions.*

EXERCISE 38   Trees in Swing. (Challenging).

In Swing, JTree is in the javax.swing package, and TreeModel and DefaultTreeModel are in the javax.swing.tree package. (The table classes have a similar organization.)

EXERCISE 38   Trees in Swing. (Challenging). (Continued)

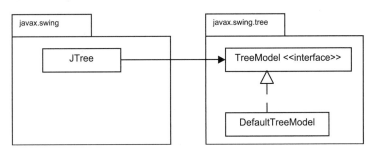

A. **Explain how the TreeModel interface breaks the dependency between JTree and DefaultTreeModel.**

B. **Explain how there are still dependencies at the package level.**

C. **Suppose each package corresponds to a library (this is an oversimplification). Explain a way to break the package dependency so that JTree could be shipped in a library independent of DefaultTreeModel.**

D. **Systems today ship with so much disk space; why should anybody worry about library dependencies?**

■ *See Appendix A for solutions.*

11

ACCOMMODATING CHANGE

Some problems become most apparent when you try to change your code. (Most of the other smells we've discussed can be detected by looking at the code statically.)

Ideally, one changed decision affects only one place in the code. When it doesn't work out that way, it's a sign of duplication in the code.

Addressing these smells often has a side benefit: Many times it makes the code easier to test.

Smells Covered

- Divergent Change
- Shotgun Surgery
- Parallel Inheritance Hierarchies
- Combinatorial Explosion

Divergent Change

Symptoms

- You find yourself changing the same class for different reasons. (For contrast, see *Shotgun Surgery*, the next smell we look at.)

Causes

The class picks up more responsibilities as it evolves, with no one noticing that two different types of decisions are involved. (Recall in Chapter 6 we talked about Parnas's dictum that a module should have only one secret.)

What to Do

- If the class both finds an object and does something with it, let the caller find the object and pass it in, or let the class return a value that the caller uses.
- *Extract Class* to pull out separate classes for the separate decisions.
- If several classes are sharing the same type of decisions, you may be able to consolidate those new classes (e.g., by *Extract Superclass* or *Extract Subclass*). In the limit, these classes can form a layer (e.g., a persistence layer).

Payoff

Improves communication (by expressing intent better). Improves robustness to future changes.

Contraindications

None identified.

EXERCISE 39   CsvWriter.

Consider this code to write Comma-Separated Value (CSV) files. (Online at *http://www.xp123.com/rwb*)

CsvWriter.java

```java
public class CsvWriter {
    public CsvWriter() {}

    public void write(String[][] lines) {
        for (int i = 0; i < lines.length; i++)
            writeLine(lines[i]);
    }

    private void writeLine(String[] fields) {
        if (fields.length == 0)
            System.out.println();
        else {
            writeField(fields[0]);

            for (int i = 1; i < fields.length; i++) {
                System.out.print(",");
                writeField(fields[i]);
            }
            System.out.println();
        }
    }
}
```

EXERCISE 39 CsvWriter. (Continued)

```java
    private void writeField(String field) {
        if (field.indexOf(',') != -1 || field.indexOf('\"') != -1)
            writeQuoted(field);
        else
            System.out.print(field);
    }

    private void writeQuoted(String field) {
        System.out.print('\"');
        for (int i = 0; i < field.length(); i++) {
            char c = field.charAt(i);
            if (c == '\"')
                System.out.print("\"\"");
            else
                System.out.print(c);
        }
        System.out.print('\"');
    }
}
```

CsvWriterTest.java (A Manual Test)

```java
import junit.framework.TestCase;

public class CsvWriterTest extends TestCase {
    public CsvWriterTest (String name) {
        super(name);
    }

    public void testWriter() {
        CsvWriter writer = new CsvWriter();
        String[] [] lines = new String[] [] {
    new String[] {},
    new String[] {"only one field"},
    new String[] {"two", "fields"},
    new String[] {"", "contents", "several words included"},
    new String[] {",", "embedded , commas, included", "trailing comma,"},
    new String[] {"\"", "embedded \" quotes",
        "multiple \"\"\" quotes\"\""},
    new String[] {"mixed commas, and \"quotes\"", "simple field"}
        };

        // Expected:
        //                          -- (empty line)
        // only one field
        // two,fields
        // ,contents,several words included
        // ",","embedded , commas, included","trailing comma,"
```

EXERCISE 39   CsvWriter. (Continued)

```
        // """","embedded "" quotes","multiple """""" quotes""""""
        // "mixed commas, and ""quotes""",simple field

        writer.write(lines);
    }
}
```

A. **How is this code an example of divergent change? (What decisions does it embody?)**

B. **Modify this code to write to a stream passed in as an argument.**

C. **Starting from the original code, modify the functions to return a string value corresponding to what the functions would have written.**

D. **Which version seems better and why? Which is easier to test?**

■ *See Appendix A for solutions.*

EXERCISE 40   CheckingAccount.

Consider these class fragments:

```
public class CheckingAccount {
    public int balance() {…}
    public void add(Transaction transaction) {…}
}

public class Transaction {
    public int cost() {…}
}
```

EXERCISE 40 CheckingAccount. (Continued)

> ### A. What decisions are embedded in these classes?
>
>
>
> ### B. Extract a simple Money class.
>
>
>
> ▪ *See Appendix A for solutions.*

Shotgun Surgery

Symptoms

- Making a simple change requires you to change several classes.

Causes

One responsibility is split among several classes. There may be a missing class that would understand the whole responsibility (and which would get a cluster of changes). Or, this can happen through an overzealous attempt to eliminate Divergent Change.

What to Do

- Identify the class that should own the group of changes. It may be an existing class, or you may need to *Extract Class* to create a new one.
- Use *Move Field* and *Move Method* to put the functionality onto the chosen class. Once the class not chosen is simple enough, you may be able to use *Inline Class* to eliminate that class.

Payoff

Reduces duplication. Improves communication. Improves maintainability (as future changes will be more localized).

Contraindications

None identified.

EXERCISE 41 Shotgun Surgery.

> In code you have access to, find examples of this problem. Some frequent candidates:
>
> • **Configuration information.**
>
> • **Logging.**
>
> • **Persistence.**
>
> • **Sometimes it takes two calls on an object to get something common done, and this two-step process is used in several places.**

Parallel Inheritance Hierarchies

Symptoms

- You make a new subclass in one hierarchy, and find yourself required to create a related subclass in another hierarchy.
- You find two hierarchies where the subclasses have the same prefix. (The naming reflects the requirement to coordinate hierarchies.)

This is a special case of *Shotgun Surgery*, discussed earlier.

Causes

The hierarchies probably grew in parallel, a class and its pair being needed at the same time. As usual, it probably wasn't bad at first, but after two or more pairs get introduced, it becomes too complicated to change one thing. (Often both classes embody different aspects of the same decision.)

What to Do

- Use *Move Field* and *Move Method* to redistribute the features in such a way that you can eliminate one of the hierarchies.

Payoff

Reduces duplication. May improve communication. May reduce size.

Contraindications

None identified. (This smell may happen along the way from improving a particularly tangled situation.)

EXERCISE 42 Duplicate Observed Data.

> *Duplicate Observed Data* splits a class in two—one part model, the other part view. (For example, it might turn Card into CardModel and CardView.) It is often natural for the model classes to form a hierarchy (they have similar notification needs), and it's natural for the views to form a hierarchy (they all display). This sounds like a Parallel Inheritance Hierarchy. Is it a problem?
>
> ■ *See Appendix A for solutions.*

Combinatorial Explosion

This is a relative of Parallel Inheritance Hierarchies, but everything has been folded into one hierarchy.

Symptoms

- You want to introduce a single new class, but it turns out that you have to introduce multiple classes at various points of the hierarchy.
- You notice that each layer of the hierarchy uses a common set of words (e.g., one level adds style information, and the next adds mutability).

Causes

What should be independent decisions instead get implemented via a hierarchy.

What to Do

- If things aren't too far gone, you may be able to *Replace Inheritance with Delegation.* (By keeping the same interface for the variants, you can create an example of the Decorator design pattern.)

- If the situation has grown too complex, you're in big refactoring territory and can *Tease Apart Inheritance* (see Fowler's *Refactoring* for the details).

Payoff

Reduces duplication. Reduces size.

Contraindications

None identified.

EXERCISE 43   Documents.

Consider this hierarchy:

```
Document
    AsciiDocument
        ZippedAsciiDocument
        RawAsciiDocument
            BriefAsciiDocument
    HtmlDocument
        RawHtmlDocument
        ZippedHtmlDocument
    MarcDocument
        BriefMarcDocument
        FullMarcDocument
```

A. **What's the impact of adding a new compression type that all document types will support?**

B. **Rearrange the hierarchy so it's based first on compression (or none), then brief/full, then document type. Is this an improvement?**

C. **Describe a different approach, using the Decorator pattern.**

■ *See Appendix A for solutions.*

12

LIBRARY CLASSES

A modern application will use library classes.

Library classes sometimes put us in a dilemma. We want the library to be different, but we don't want to change it. Even when it's possible to change a library, it carries risks: It affects other clients, and it means we have to redo our changes for future versions of the library.

Smells Covered

- Incomplete Library Class

Incomplete Library Class

Symptoms

- You're using a library class, and there's a feature you wish were on that class, but it's not. If it were a normal class, you'd modify it; but, since it is part of a library, you may be unable or unwilling to change it.

Causes

The author of the library class didn't anticipate your need (or declined to support it due to other trade-offs).

What to Do

- See if the owner of the class or library will consider adding the support you want.

- If it's just one or two methods, *Introduce Foreign Method* on a client of the library class. (This is still Feature Envy, but what can you do?)
- If you have several methods, *Introduce Local Extension* (subclassing the library class to create a new pseudo-library class). Use the new extension class going forward.
- You may decide to introduce a layer covering the library.

Payoff

Reduces duplication (when you can reuse library code instead of implementing it completely from scratch).

Contraindications

If several projects each use incompatible ways to extend a library, this can lead to extra work if the library changes.

Challenges

EXERCISE 44   Layers. (Challenging).

One way to deal with libraries is to put them beneath a layer. This lets you isolate the bulk of your code from direct dependency on other libraries. Consider these two alternatives:

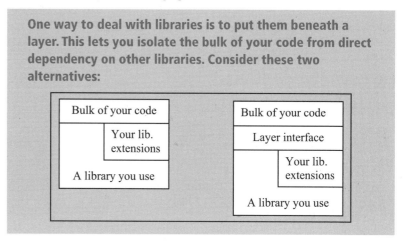

EXERCISE 44 Layers. (Challenging). (Continued)

A. Redraw this as a UML package diagram showing dependencies.

B. Explain how the bulk of your code does or does not depend on the library code in each of these situations.

C. What effects does this layering have in terms of:

- Conceptual integrity?
- Portability?
- Performance?
- Testing?

D. What mechanisms do you have available to enforce the layering (that is, what stops someone from turning the second approach into the first one)?

■ *See Appendix A for solutions.*

EXERCISE 45 Trees.

The Swing tree library (see javax.swing.tree.*) has an interesting flaw. This library has the idea of a DefaultTreeModel (class) built out of MutableTreeNodes (interface) objects. Although there is a DefaultMutableTreeNode class, you might not want to use it if you already have node-like objects. (You might prefer to implement the MutableTreeNode interface rather than copy your information to a DefaultMutableTreeNode.)

EXERCISE 45   Trees. (Continued)

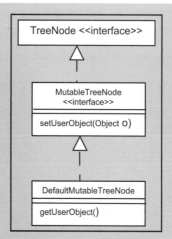

The flaw in the library is a gap in the MutableTreeNode interface: It supports a method `setUserObject()`, **but no method** `getUserObject()`.

Suppose you'd like to have this method.

    A. Does Introduce Foreign Method or Introduce Local Extension seem more appropriate? Why?

■ *See Appendix A for solutions.*

EXERCISE 46   String

    A. The String class in Java is declared *final.* **What effect does this have on** *Introduce Local Extension*?

    B. Why would the creators of Java make String final?

■ *See Appendix A for solutions.*

EXERCISE 47   Filter. (Challenging).

The Collections class in java.util defines a number of utility methods, including one to produce an enumeration for a collection. This enumerator gives a list of all elements, but it doesn't provide a way to filter them.

A. Write a class to wrap Enumerator, extending it with the ability to return objects that meet some criteria. (Include tests.)

B. What parent class or interface does your class have (if any)?

C. What arguments does the constructor take (if any)?

D. What methods does it define?

■ *See Appendix A for solutions.*

EXERCISE 48   Diagrams. (Challenging).

Draw class or other UML diagrams to help explain and show the difference between *Introduce Foreign Method*, *Introduce Local Extension*, layering, and wrapping.

■ *See Appendix A for solutions.*

EXERCISE 49   A Missing Function.

> Consider the Zumbacker Z function, at the core of your application. (In fact, it's such a commonly used function in your domain that you're a little surprised it's not in the Java math libraries already.) It's defined:
>
> $Z(x) = abs[\ cos(x) + sin(x) - exp(x)\ ]$
>
> How could you handle the problem of java.lang.Math being an incomplete library?

■ *See Appendix A for solutions.*

INTERLUDE 4 GEN-A-REFACTORING

Several refactorings have the form "Verb Noun."

Consider these verbs: Extract, Inline; Move; Rename; Pull Up, Push Down; Hide, Expose.

Consider these nouns: Field, Method; Class, Interface, Subclass, Superclass; Hierarchy.

INTERLUDE I4.1 Verbs and Nouns.

In the table below, put a dash (—) in combinations that don't make sense, a plus sign (+) in those that are in Fowler's *Refactoring* catalog, and an asterisk (*) in those that make sense but aren't in the catalog.

	Extract	Inline	Move	Rename	Pull Up	Push Down	Hide	Expose
Field								
Method								
Class								
Interface								
Subclass								
Superclass								
Hierarchy								

■ *See Appendix A for solution.*

SECTION 3

PROGRAMS TO REFACTOR

13

A DATABASE EXAMPLE

Reggie is a system to handle course registration for a small school.

The developers are using a database to maintain information about students and classes. The first version of the database is simple (see Figure 13.1).

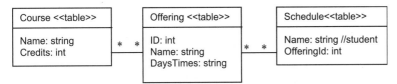

FIGURE 13.1 School Registration Database—First Version

A Course is a class that could be offered. For now, we'll use simple names ("Econ101" for "Introduction to Economics"). Later, this will expand to include a full title, description, and other information about the course.

An Offering is a version of a class, taught on some schedule. DaysTimes is a comma-separated string of days and times ("M10,T11,F10"). Again, there will be more information added in development.

A Schedule is a particular set of offerings that a student has chosen. There are rules about how schedules can be formed:

- At least 12 credits
- At most 18 credits, unless an overload is authorized
- No conflicting times
- No duplicate courses

Rather than being enforced by the database, these rules are enforced by code that checks schedules.

EXERCISE 50   Data Smells.

> Refactoring deals mostly with code smells. But there are data smells too; the database community has notions of what constitutes a good data design.
>
> A. What potential problems do you see in this database structure?
>
> B. What changes to the database might address them? (Don't make the changes yet.)
>
> ■ *See Appendix A for solutions.*

In the code below, there are three classes corresponding to the tables. They start out small and perhaps are a little too focused on the data, but they're much bigger with database code added. For an introduction to database programming in Java, see the JDBC Database Access trail of the Java Tutorial (*java.sun.com/docs/books/tutorial/jdbc*) or the JDBC Short Course (*developer.java.sun.com/developer/onlineTraining/Database/JDBCShortCourse*). The code uses the JDBC-ODBC driver to talk to a text-file database.

Course.java (Online at *www.xp123.com/rwb*)

```java
import java.sql.*;

public class Course {
    private String name;
    private int credits;
    static String url = "jdbc:odbc:Reggie";

    static { try { Class.forName("sun.jdbc.odbc.JdbcOdbcDriver"); }
            catch (Exception ignored) {} }
```

```java
public static Course create(String name, int credits)
    throws Exception
{
  Connection conn = null;

  try {
      conn = DriverManager.getConnection(url, "", "");
      Statement statement = conn.createStatement();
      statement.executeUpdate(
          "DELETE FROM course WHERE name = '" + name + "';");
      statement.executeUpdate(
          "INSERT INTO course VALUES ('" + name
          + "', '" + credits + "');");
      return new Course(name, credits);
  } finally {
      try { conn.close(); } catch (Exception ignored) {}
  }
}

public static Course find(String name) {
    Connection conn = null;
    try {
        conn = DriverManager.getConnection(url, "", "");
        Statement statement = conn.createStatement();
        ResultSet result = statement.executeQuery(
            "SELECT * FROM course WHERE Name = '" + name + "';");
        if (!result.next()) return null;

        int credits = result.getInt("Credits");
        return new Course(name, credits);
    } catch (Exception ex) {
        return null;
    } finally {
        try { conn.close(); } catch (Exception ignored) {}
    }
}

public void update() throws Exception {
    Connection conn = null;

    try {
        conn = DriverManager.getConnection(url, "", "");
        Statement statement = conn.createStatement();

        statement.executeUpdate(
            "DELETE FROM COURSE WHERE name = '" + name + "';");
        statement.executeUpdate(
            "INSERT INTO course VALUES('" +
            name + "','" + credits + "');");
    } finally {
        try { conn.close(); } catch (Exception ignored) {}
```

```
        }
    }

    Course(String name, int credits) {
        this.name = name;
        this.credits = credits;
    }

    public int getCredits() {
        return credits;
    }

    public String getName() {
        return name;
    }
}
```

Offering.java

```
import java.sql.*;

public class Offering {
    private int id;
    private Course course;
    private String daysTimes;

    static String url = "jdbc:odbc:Reggie";

    static { try { Class.forName("sun.jdbc.odbc.JdbcOdbcDriver"); }
            catch (Exception ignored) {} }

    public static Offering create(Course course, String daysTimesCsv)
        throws Exception
    {
        Connection conn = null;

        try {
            conn = DriverManager.getConnection(url, "", "");
            Statement statement = conn.createStatement();

            ResultSet result = statement.executeQuery(
                "SELECT MAX(ID) FROM offering;");
            result.next();
            int newId = 1 + result.getInt(1);

            statement.executeUpdate("INSERT INTO offering VALUES ('"
                    + newId + "','" + course.getName()
                    + "','" + daysTimesCsv + "');");
            return new Offering(newId, course, daysTimesCsv);
        } finally {
```

```java
            try { conn.close(); } catch (Exception ignored) {}
        }
    }

    public static Offering find(int id) {
        Connection conn = null;

        try {
            conn = DriverManager.getConnection(url, "", "");
            Statement statement = conn.createStatement();
            ResultSet result = statement.executeQuery(
                "SELECT * FROM offering WHERE ID =" + id + ";");
            if (result.next() == false)
                return null;

            String courseName = result.getString("Course");
            Course course = Course.find(courseName);
            String dateTime = result.getString("DateTime");
            conn.close();

            return new Offering(id, course, dateTime);
        } catch (Exception ex) {
            try { conn.close(); } catch (Exception ignored) {}
            return null;
        }
    }

    public void update() throws Exception {
        Connection conn = null;

        try {
            conn = DriverManager.getConnection(url, "", "");
            Statement statement = conn.createStatement();

            statement.executeUpdate(
                "DELETE FROM Offering WHERE ID=" + id + ";");
            statement.executeUpdate(
                    "INSERT INTO Offering VALUES('" + id + "','" +
                        course.getName() + "','" + daysTimes + "');");
        } finally {
            try { conn.close(); } catch (Exception ignored) {}
        }
    }

    public Offering(int id, Course course, String daysTimesCsv) {
        this.id = id;
        this.course = course;
        this.daysTimes = daysTimesCsv;
    }
```

```java
    public int getId() {
        return id;
    }

    public Course getCourse() {
        return course;
    }

    public String getDaysTimes() {
        return daysTimes;
    }

    public String toString() {
        return "Offering " + getId() + ": "
+ getCourse() + " meeting " + getDaysTimes();
    }
}
```

Schedule.java

```java
import java.util.*;
import java.sql.*;

public class Schedule {
    String name;
    int credits = 0;
    static final int minCredits = 12;
    static final int maxCredits = 18;
    boolean overloadAuthorized = false;
    ArrayList schedule = new ArrayList();

    static String url = "jdbc:odbc:Reggie";
    static { try { Class.forName("sun.jdbc.odbc.JdbcOdbcDriver"); }
            catch (Exception ignored) {} }

    public static void deleteAll() throws Exception {
        Connection conn = null;

        try {
            conn = DriverManager.getConnection(url, "", "");
            Statement statement = conn.createStatement();

            statement.executeUpdate("DELETE * FROM schedule;");
        } finally {
            try { conn.close(); } catch (Exception ignored) {}
        }
    }

    public static Schedule create(String name) throws Exception {
        Connection conn = null;
```

```java
        try {
            conn = DriverManager.getConnection(url, "", "");
            Statement statement = conn.createStatement();

            statement.executeUpdate(
                "DELETE FROM schedule WHERE name = '" + name + "';");
            return new Schedule(name);
        } finally {
            try { conn.close(); } catch (Exception ignored) {}
        }
    }

    public static Schedule find(String name) {
        Connection conn = null;

        try {
            conn = DriverManager.getConnection(url, "", "");
            Statement statement = conn.createStatement();
            ResultSet result = statement.executeQuery(
                "SELECT * FROM schedule WHERE Name= '" + name + "';");

            Schedule schedule = new Schedule(name);

            while (result.next()) {
                int offeringId = result.getInt("OfferingId");
                Offering offering = Offering.find(offeringId);
                schedule.add(offering);
            }

            return schedule;
        } catch (Exception ex) {
            return null;
        } finally {
            try { conn.close(); } catch (Exception ignored) {}
        }
    }

    public static Collection all() throws Exception {
        ArrayList result = new ArrayList();
        Connection conn = null;

        try {
            conn = DriverManager.getConnection(url, "", "");
            Statement statement = conn.createStatement();
            ResultSet results = statement.executeQuery(
                "SELECT DISTINCT Name FROM schedule;");

            while (results.next())
                result.add(Schedule.find(results.getString("Name")));
        } finally {
            try { conn.close(); } catch (Exception ignored) {}
```

```
        }

        return result;
    }

    public void update() throws Exception {
        Connection conn = null;

        try {
            conn = DriverManager.getConnection(url, "", "");
            Statement statement = conn.createStatement();

            statement.executeUpdate(
                "DELETE FROM schedule WHERE name = '" + name + "';");

            for (int i = 0; i < schedule.size(); i++) {
                Offering offering = (Offering) schedule.get(i);
                statement.executeUpdate(
                    "INSERT INTO schedule VALUES('" + name + "','"
                    + offering.getId() + "');");
            }
        } finally {
            try { conn.close(); } catch (Exception ignored) {}
        }
    }

    public Schedule(String name) {
        this.name = name;
    }

    public void add(Offering offering) {
        credits += offering.getCourse().getCredits();
        schedule.add(offering);
    }

    public void authorizeOverload(boolean authorized) {
        overloadAuthorized = authorized;
    }

    public List analysis() {
        ArrayList result = new ArrayList();

        if (credits < minCredits)
            result.add("Too few credits");

        if (credits > maxCredits && !overloadAuthorized)
            result.add("Too many credits");

        checkDuplicateCourses(result);

        checkOverlap(result);
```

```java
            return result;
    }

    public void checkDuplicateCourses(ArrayList analysis) {
        HashSet courses = new HashSet();
        for (int i = 0; i < schedule.size(); i++) {
            Course course = ((Offering) schedule.get(i)).getCourse();
            if (courses.contains(course))
                analysis.add("Same course twice - " + course.getName());
            courses.add(course);
        }
    }

    public void checkOverlap(ArrayList analysis) {
      HashSet times = new HashSet();

      for (Iterator iterator = schedule.iterator();
          iterator.hasNext();)
      {
          Offering offering = (Offering) iterator.next();
          String daysTimes = offering.getDaysTimes();
          StringTokenizer tokens = new StringTokenizer(daysTimes, ",");
          while (tokens.hasMoreTokens()) {
              String dayTime = tokens.nextToken();
              if (times.contains(dayTime))
                  analysis.add("Course overlap - " + dayTime);
              times.add(dayTime);
          }
      }
    }

    public String toString() {
        return "Schedule " + name + ": " + schedule;
    }
}
```

Report.java

```java
import java.util.*;

public class Report {
    public Report() {
    }

    Hashtable offeringToName = new Hashtable();

    public void populateMap() throws Exception {
        Collection schedules = Schedule.all();
        for (Iterator eachSchedule = schedules.iterator();
            eachSchedule.hasNext();)
        {
```

```java
            Schedule schedule = (Schedule) eachSchedule.next();

            for (Iterator each = schedule.schedule.iterator();
                each.hasNext(); )
            {
                Offering offering = (Offering) each.next();
                populateMapFor(schedule, offering);
            }
        }
    }

    private void populateMapFor(Schedule schedule, Offering offering) {
        ArrayList list = (ArrayList) offeringToName.get(
            new Integer(offering.getId()));
        if (list == null) {
            list = new ArrayList();
            offeringToName.put(new Integer(offering.getId()), list);
        }
        list.add(schedule.name);
    }

    public void writeOffering(
        StringBuffer buffer, ArrayList list, Offering offering)
    {
        buffer.append(offering.getCourse().getName() + " "
                    + offering.getDaysTimes() + "\n");

        for (Iterator iterator = list.iterator(); iterator.hasNext();)
        {
            String s = (String) iterator.next();
            buffer.append("\t" + s + "\n");
        }
    }

    public void write(StringBuffer buffer) throws Exception {
        populateMap();

        Enumeration enumeration = offeringToName.keys();
        while (enumeration.hasMoreElements()) {
            Integer offeringId = (Integer) enumeration.nextElement();
            ArrayList list = (ArrayList) offeringToName.get(offeringId);
            writeOffering(buffer, list,
                Offering.find(offeringId.intValue()));
        }

        buffer.append("Number of scheduled offerings: ");
        buffer.append(offeringToName.size());
        buffer.append("\n");
    }
}
```

TestSchedule.java

```java
import junit.framework.TestCase;
import java.util.List;
import java.util.Collection;

public class TestSchedule extends TestCase {
    public TestSchedule(String name) {
        super(name);
    }

    public void testMinCredits() {
        Schedule schedule = new Schedule("name");
        Collection analysis = schedule.analysis();
        assertEquals(1, analysis.size());
        assertTrue(analysis.contains("Too few credits"));
    }

    public void testJustEnoughCredits() {
        Course cs110 = new Course("CS110", 11);
        Offering mwf10 = new Offering(1, cs110, "M10,W10,F10");
        Schedule schedule = new Schedule("name");
        schedule.add(mwf10);
        List analysis = schedule.analysis();
        assertEquals(1, analysis.size());
        assertTrue(analysis.contains("Too few credits"));

        schedule = new Schedule("name");
        Course cs101 = new Course("CS101", 12);
        Offering th11 = new Offering(1, cs101, "T11,H11");
        schedule.add(th11);
        analysis = schedule.analysis();
        assertEquals(0, analysis.size());
    }

    public void testMaxCredits() {
        Course cs110 = new Course("CS110", 20);
        Offering mwf10 = new Offering(1, cs110, "M10,W10,F10");
        Schedule schedule = new Schedule("name");
        schedule.add(mwf10);
        List analysis = schedule.analysis();
        assertEquals(1, analysis.size());
        assertTrue(analysis.contains("Too many credits"));

        schedule.authorizeOverload(true);
        analysis = schedule.analysis();
        assertEquals(0, analysis.size());
    }
```

```java
public void testJustBelowMax() {
    Course cs110 = new Course("CS110", 19);
    Offering mwf10 = new Offering(1, cs110, "M10,W10,F10");
    Schedule schedule = new Schedule("name");
    schedule.add(mwf10);
    List analysis = schedule.analysis();
    assertEquals(1, analysis.size());
    assertTrue(analysis.contains("Too many credits"));

    schedule = new Schedule("name");
    Course cs101 = new Course("CS101", 18);
    Offering th11 = new Offering(1, cs101, "T11,H11");
    schedule.add(th11);
    analysis = schedule.analysis();
    assertEquals(0, analysis.size());
}

public void testDupCourses() {
    Course cs110 = new Course("CS110", 6);
    Offering mwf10 = new Offering(1, cs110, "M10,W10,F10");
    Offering th11 = new Offering(1, cs110, "T11,H11");
    Schedule schedule = new Schedule("name");
    schedule.add(mwf10);
    schedule.add(th11);
    List analysis = schedule.analysis();
    assertEquals(1, analysis.size());
    assertTrue(analysis.contains("Same course twice - CS110"));
}

public void testOverlap() {
    Schedule schedule = new Schedule("name");

    Course cs110 = new Course("CS110", 6);
    Offering mwf10 = new Offering(1, cs110, "M10,W10,F10");
    schedule.add(mwf10);

    Course cs101 = new Course("CS101", 6);
    Offering mixed = new Offering(1, cs101, "M10,W11,F11");
    schedule.add(mixed);

    List analysis = schedule.analysis();
    assertEquals(1, analysis.size());
    assertTrue(analysis.contains("Course overlap - M10"));

    Course cs102 = new Course("CS102", 1);
    Offering mixed2 = new Offering(1, cs102, "M9,W10,F11");
    schedule.add(mixed2);

    analysis = schedule.analysis();
    assertEquals(3, analysis.size());
    assertTrue(analysis.contains("Course overlap - M10"));
```

```java
        assertTrue(analysis.contains("Course overlap - W10"));
        assertTrue(analysis.contains("Course overlap - F11"));
    }
    public void testCourseCreate() throws Exception {
        Course c = Course.create("CS202", 1);

        Course c2 = Course.find("CS202");
        assertEquals("CS202", c2.getName());

        Course c3 = Course.find("Nonexistent");
        assertNull(c3);
    }

    public void testOfferingCreate() throws Exception {
        Course c = Course.create("CS202", 2);
        Offering offering = Offering.create(c, "M10");
        assertNotNull(offering);
    }

    public void testPersistentSchedule() throws Exception {
        Schedule s = Schedule.create("Bob");
        assertNotNull(s);
    }

    public void testScheduleUpdate() throws Exception {
        Course cs101 = Course.create("CS101", 3);
        cs101.update();
        Offering off1 = Offering.create(cs101, "M10");
        off1.update();
        Offering off2 = Offering.create(cs101, "T9");
        off2.update();

        Schedule s = Schedule.create("Bob");
        s.add(off1);
        s.add(off2);
        s.update();

        Schedule s2 = Schedule.create("Alice");
        s2.add(off1);
        s2.update();

        Schedule s3 = Schedule.find("Bob");
        assertEquals(2, s3.schedule.size());

        Schedule s4 = Schedule.find("Alice");
        assertEquals(1, s4.schedule.size());
    }
}
```

TestReport.java

```java
import junit.framework.TestCase;

import java.util.List;
import java.util.Collection;

public class TestReport extends TestCase {
    public TestReport(String name) { super(name); }

    public void testEmptyReport() throws Exception {
        Schedule.deleteAll();
        Report report = new Report();

        StringBuffer buffer = new StringBuffer();

        report.write(buffer);

        assertEquals(
            "Number of scheduled offerings: 0\n",
            buffer.toString());
    }

    public void testReport() throws Exception {
        Schedule.deleteAll();

        Course cs101 = Course.create("CS101", 3);
        cs101.update();
        Offering off1 = Offering.create(cs101, "M10");
        off1.update();
        Offering off2 = Offering.create(cs101, "T9");
        off2.update();

        Schedule s = Schedule.create("Bob");
        s.add(off1);
        s.add(off2);
        s.update();

        Schedule s2 = Schedule.create("Alice");
        s2.add(off1);
        s2.update();

        Report report = new Report();

        StringBuffer buffer = new StringBuffer();

        report.write(buffer);
```

```
       String result = buffer.toString();
       String valid1 = "CS101 M10\n\tAlice\n\tBob\n" +
                       "CS101 T9\n\tBob\n" +
                       "Number of scheduled offerings: 2\n";

       String valid2 = "CS101 T9\n\tBob\n" +
                       "CS101 M10\n\tAlice\n\tBob\n" +
                       "Number of scheduled offerings: 2\n";
       assertTrue(result.equals(valid1) || result.equals(valid2));
    }
}
```

EXERCISE 51   Duplication. (Challenging).

A. **Identify smells, especially the duplication (and the differences!) between these classes.**

B. **What is the pattern of access for persistence? (That is, trace the life of an object from creation to destruction.)**

■ *See Appendix A for solutions.*

EXERCISE 52   Application. (Challenging).

A. **The database-related routines are tantalizingly similar. Apply refactorings that will reduce this duplication.**

B. **Create a class that provides the bulk of the database support. Should this be a parent of these objects or a separate class?**

■ *See Appendix A for solutions.*

EXERCISE 53   Database Layer. (Challenging).

In the refactorings you just performed, one effect has been to move the code toward a database layer.

A. What extra work would you have to do to create an in-memory version of the database classes?

B. Why might you want to do this?

C. How much of the JDBC would be exposed by your new layer?

■ *See Appendix A for solutions.*

For more information on creating a database layer, see J2EE (tool support for automatic mapping of Enterprise Java Beans [EJBs]), WebGain TopLink (see *www.webgain.com/products/toplink/*), or Scott Ambler's description (*www.ambysoft.com/mappingObjects.html*). One thing these references will show you is that you may not want to undertake lightly the development of a full-fledged layer.

EXERCISE 54   Find.

The find() routines create a new instance of an object even if it's already been *found* before.

A. Make find() cache its objects, returning a previously found object if possible.

EXERCISE 54   Find. (Continued)

B. Is this refactoring or development? Did you add tests to verify the new behavior? (You should.)

C. The Report makes it a point to store *keys* of offerings. Use the improved nature of find() to simplify the report's code.

■ *See Appendix A for solutions.*

EXERCISE 55   Multiple Open Queries.

Some databases have a restriction that a connection can't have multiple queries *open* at the same time. (An example occurs in Schedule.find(): While building a Schedule, it queries Offerings.find(), which also queries the database.)

A. How much code (and in how many places) would be affected by a change to enforce this discipline?

B. The *naïve* approach used in this code instantiates all related objects for each row that is loaded. How else might you do it?

■ *See Appendix A for solutions.*

EXERCISE 56   Counter.

The counter in Offering is manipulated in a two-step process: Get the current max value of the counter in any row and create a new row with an ID one bigger. When will this strategy be inadequate? What could you do about it?

■ *See Appendix A for solutions.*

EXERCISE 57   Report.

The Report creates a list of offerings and the students in each.

A. Write a structured query language (SQL) query (if you know SQL) to produce the information in this report.

B. What are the trade-offs between the two approaches?

EXERCISE 58   Database Refactorings. (Challenging).

Earlier, we described some possible database changes: introducing IDs (rather than using string keys), extracting a new table, and so on. We can't just make these changes in the database; our code depends on the database structure, so the changes must be coordinated.

A. Describe Rename Column as a refactoring. Tell what to change in the database or the code, when to change it, when to run tests, and so on.

EXERCISE 58   Database Refactorings. (Challenging). (Continued)

B. **Describe Split Table (turning one table into two related tables) as a refactoring. Make sure you account for any data migration.**

C. **Are there intermediate steps that could temporarily leave the database in a slightly worse structure, but at the same time could make the overall refactoring safer? (Think of how Extract Method copies and adjusts the new method before deleting the old one, or how some refactorings change things one at a time, running tests after each change.)**

■ *See Appendix A for solutions.*

EXERCISE 59   Domain Class Independence.

Suggest ways in which the domain classes could be made more independent of the database access part of these classes.

■ *See Appendix A for solutions.*

14

A SIMPLE GAME

This example involves refactoring and test-driven design.

Suppose we've decided to develop a system to play games in the tic-tac-toe family: squares occupied by different markers. In tic-tac-toe, you have a 3×3 grid, and you try to put your mark in three boxes in a row. In Connect Four by Hasbro, you have a rectangular grid and try to get four boxes in a row, but columns have to be filled from bottom to top. We'll start with a simplified version of tic-tac-toe and work our way up to the general case.

Here are some tests and the first version of the code (online at *www.xp123.com/rwb*).

```
import junit.framework.*;

public class GameTest extends TestCase {

    public GameTest(String s) {super(s);}

    public void testDefaultMove() {
        Game game = new Game("XOXOX-OXO");
        assertEquals(5, game.move('X'));

        game = new Game("XOXOXOOX-");
        assertEquals(8, game.move('O'));

        game = new Game("---------");
        assertEquals(0, game.move('X'));

        game = new Game("XXXXXXXXX");
        assertEquals(-1, game.move('X'));
    }

    public void testFindWinningMove() {
        Game game = new Game("XO-XX-OOX");
        assertEquals(5, game.move('X'));
    }
    public void testWinConditions() {
        Game game = new Game("---XXX---");
```

```java
        assertEquals('X', game.winner());
    }
}

public class Game {
    public StringBuffer board;

    public Game(String s) {board = new StringBuffer(s);}

    public Game(StringBuffer s, int position, char player) {
        board = new StringBuffer();
        board.append(s);
        board.setCharAt(position, player);
    }

    public int move(char player) {
        for (int i = 0; i < 9; i++) {
            if (board.charAt(i) == '-') {
                Game game = play(i, player);
                if (game.winner() == player)
                    return i;
            }
        }

        for (int i = 0; i < 9; i++) {
            if (board.charAt(i) == '-')
                return i;
        }
        return -1;
    }

    public Game play(int i, char player) {
        return new Game(this.board, i, player);
    }

    public char winner() {
        if (board.charAt(0) != '-'
                && board.charAt(0) == board.charAt(1)
                && board.charAt(1) == board.charAt(2))
            return board.charAt(0);
        if (board.charAt(3) != '-'
                && board.charAt(3) == board.charAt(4)
                && board.charAt(4) == board.charAt(5))
            return board.charAt(3);
        if (board.charAt(6) != '-'
                && board.charAt(6) == board.charAt(7)
                && board.charAt(7) == board.charAt(8))
            return board.charAt(6);
        return '-';
    }
}
```

Notice that the `winner()` routine is simplified: You win by getting three in a row horizontally. Notice also that the heuristics for what to play are primitive: Win if you can, play anything otherwise. We'll migrate toward something capable of more sophisticated strategies.

EXERCISE 60   Smells.

> **Go through this code and identify smells.**
>
> ■ *See Appendix A for solutions.*

EXERCISE 61   Easy Changes.

> **It's not always easy to know what to do with code. Let's fix some of the easy things first. Fix them one at a time.**
>
> - **The variable** i **doesn't explain much either. Change it to** move**.**
>
> - **The value** -1 **is a flag value; create a constant** NoMove **to represent it.**
>
> - **The** winner() **function has a lot of duplication. Eliminate the duplication.**
>
> - **The check for a board character being a '-' is really a check that the square is unoccupied. Extract a method to do this, and name it appropriately.**

We have two "for" loops—one to find a winning move, the other to find a default move. One way to handle this would be to extract each one into a method. As we add more strategies, we could see each strategy getting its own method. An alternative would be to merge the two loops and handle things in one pass through the possible moves. We'll take the latter approach.

One step along the way might be to assign a value to a temporary variable rather than to return it right away. You might make the second loop look like this:

```
defaultMove = NoMove;
for (int i = 0; i < 9; i++) {
   if (board[i] == '-')
```

EXERCISE 62   Fuse Loops.

> The term *Fuse Loops* means combine two loops into one. Do
> so in small steps, in such a way that you maintain safety as
> you do it. When is it safe to merge two loops? (*Fuse Loops* is
> a standard technique compilers use; it's not in Fowler's
> *Refactoring* catalog.)
>
> ■ *See Appendix A for solutions.*

```
    if (defaultMove == NoMove)
        defaultMove = i;
}
```

That is the safest approach, used because we do not want our
refactoring to change behavior. To be equivalent to the original,
we need the guard clause to make sure we haven't assigned a
defaultMove yet. But let's put on a development hat: We don't
really care which default move we make, so we could delete the
defaultMove==NoMove test. It's not necessary to stop when we find
a viable move; that is, there's no harm in trying each possible
move, provided we prefer wins to defaults. So you can delete the
break tests that exit early. Run the tests again and be sure you
haven't changed anything important. (You may have to change
the tests. What does this tell you?)

Now we have a single loop, but the condition to decide what to
return is still a little complicated:

```
if (winningMove != NoMove)
    return winningMove;
if (defaultMove != NoMove)
    return defaultMove;
return NoMove;
```

EXERCISE 63   Result.

> How would you simplify this?

EXERCISE 64   Next.

> **What refactorings would you tackle next?**

There are still a lot of *magic numbers* floating around. The winner() routine is full of them, and we still have a "9" in the main loop of bestMoveFor().

EXERCISE 65   Constants.

> **What is "9"? Name some constants and rewrite it.**

I struggled over the names, and ended up using *rows* and *columns*. (I'm also experimenting with different naming conventions; some styles might use ROWS and COLUMNS.)

EXERCISE 66   Duplication in winner().

> **Here's the winner() routine as it is now.**
>
> ```java
> public char winner() {
>    if (!canPlay(0)
>        && board.charAt(0) == board.charAt(1)
>        && board.charAt(1) == board.charAt(2))
>        return board.charAt(0);
>    if (!canPlay(3)
>          && board.charAt(3) == board.charAt(4)
>          && board.charAt(4) == board.charAt(5))
>          return board.charAt(3);
>        if (!canPlay(6)
>             && board.charAt(6) == board.charAt(7)
>             && board.charAt(7) == board.charAt(8))
>             return board.charAt(6);
>          return '-';
> }
> ```
>
> **Eliminate the duplication in this routine.**

I imagine you used a loop over the rows and extracted some sort of method that decided if there was a winning combination.

To assess your refactoring of this, switch back to a development hat. There are two changes we might make, given our vision. The first is that we're not playing tic-tac-toe yet because we're only allowing horizontal three-in-a-row wins. Extend the routine to allow vertical and diagonal wins. Was it easy to change given your refactoring?

There's another hidden constant: the number in a row that it takes to win. (Recall that we mentioned Connect Four as one of the variations we eventually want to support.) Suppose we change to a 5 × 5 grid and want four in a row to win. How easy is that to put into the code? You needn't add this feature yet; this is more of a thought question. (I gave myself a B on this one: I defined a `winningCombination()` routine that took three positions as arguments, and I created an array that explicitly called out the winning squares. This works fine for tic-tac-toe but doesn't cover *n*-in-a-row.)

Most of the refactorings we've applied so far have been obvious improvements. Now I want to grow and improve my program through a combination of refactoring and new implementation, but I'm not sure what's best to do next.

I think of this as *subjunctive programming*. The subjunctive tense is the one used to talk about possible worlds ("If I were a rich man…"). My stance is that I'll try some ideas and see where they lead, but if they don't work out, that's OK.

Two things make subjunctive programming bearable: a partner, so you can kick around ideas, and a source control system, so you can back out anything you don't like.

The general direction is that I want to allow more sophisticated strategies than "win if you can and play anything otherwise." My thought is to create a Move object and let it evaluate how good the move is.

EXERCISE 67   Iterator.

> We're running a "for" loop over the integers representing possible moves. Turn this into an iterator over the moves. This is not one of the refactorings in Fowler's *Refactoring* catalog, so let's take it in small steps.

EXERCISE 67 Iterator. (Continued)

1. **Convert from `int` to `Integer` first; that will get us into the domain of objects.**

2. **Make an iterator, where the `next()` method returns an Integer. Remove all references to `int` from the `bestMoveFor()` method.**

3. **Introduce a Move class.**

Now, the main loop looks something like this:

```
for (Iterator iter = new MoveIterator(); iter.hasNext(); ) {
    Move move = (Move)iter.next();
    if (!canPlay(move)) continue;
```

EXERCISE 68 Legal Moves Only.

Our iterator delivers all moves, legal or not. Move the canPlay test into the iterator so it delivers only legal moves.

Currently, we're just looping through possible moves, trying to select the best one, following a simple rule: Wins are best, anything else is acceptable. But wins are rare, so we'd like to pick a good intermediate move (some moves are better than others). We can think of each move as having a score: How good is it? Just to have something to work with, we'll say a win is worth 100 points and any other move is worth 0 points. (We could also think of wins by the opposing player as being worth minus 100 points (to the *home* player), but we won't check for those—yet.)

Note that we're out of the domain of refactoring; we're making a semantic change to our program. That's the way development works. Because refactoring makes things cleaner, we can see better ways to do them.

Development Episodes

EXERCISE 69 Scores.

Modify the program to calculate scores for moves and return the move with the best score.

Notice how a score is associated with a particular move. Perhaps it should be part of the Move object. Doing this might let us eliminate tracking of the integer score from the "main" loop.

EXERCISE 70   Comparing Moves.

> Add the score to the Move class. Add some sort of *max* or comparison operator between moves.

Is it better this way? It seems so to me, so I'd tentatively accept this change. But my commitment to it is not unswerving; for now, it helps, but if it gets in the way in the future, away it goes.

The program calculates every possible move and response. This is feasible for tic-tac-toe, and perhaps it's okay if we were to convert it to Hasbro's Connect Four, but it is certainly not feasible for a game like chess or Go. Eventually we would have to develop a new strategy.

One way to handle this is to limit the depth to which we search. Suppose we establish a depth cutoff value; searches deeper than this value will simply return "don't know." We will pass an additional parameter representing the current depth.

EXERCISE 71   Depth.

> Use *Add Parameter* to add a depth parameter, and maintain its value properly. Once you have the depth parameter, add an early check that returns when things are too deep. What move will you return?

EXERCISE 72   Caching.

> We can think of performance tuning as *refactoring for performance*: It tries to keep the program performing the same job, only faster. If we think of the program as exploring the game tree of possible moves, we might see the same board via different paths. Could you cache the moves, so you could recognize boards you've already rated?

EXERCISE 73 Balance.

Do we have the right balance in our objects? Are there any missing objects? Should Game calculate the score or should Move? Try shifting it around and see the consequences. Do some of these decisions make caching easier or harder?

EXERCISE 74 New Features.

Add some new features, in test-first format; make sure to refactor along the way.

    A. Score a win by the opponent at −100.

    B. Extend to mxn tic-tac-toe.

    C. Require that a move be at the lowest empty space in a column.

EXERCISE 75 Min-Max.

    A. Add another feature: Use the min-max algorithm, described in any Artificial Intelligence textbook. Instead of just saying "nonwins are all the same," you say "Choose my best move, assuming the opponent makes the move that's worst for me." The opponent uses the same rule. How is this reflected in the code? Is it a trick to use it?

EXERCISE 75   Min-Max. (Continued)

> B. There's an extension to the approach called alpha-beta pruning. It says that we can avoid searching parts of the tree by establishing cutoff values. Find an AI book and see if you can implement this approach. Is this a refactoring, a new development, or what?

EXERCISE 76   Do-Over?

> This has been an experiment in changing the structure of an application. There are other paths we could take. In particular, I feel like the balance between classes could go down a different path. Also, the first tests assumed 3 x 3 tic-tac-toe; it would be interesting to start 1 x 1 and work to m x n that way, letting 3 x 3 be a special case.
>
> Would it be better to start over, or to work from the current base?

CATALOG

"Who's in charge here?"

This is a moderate-size example involving both refactoring and development. The goal is to demonstrate how we can use refactoring to explore design decisions and their consequences.

Introduction

Imagine a store selling a variety of items. During a brief design session, we decide there are several classes of interest: Item (something for sale), Catalog (the set of all items), and Query (to find a specific set of items).

Catalog and Query must collaborate to search, but how that collaboration will occur needs to be decided. Imagine a fourth class, Interrogator. It has a method `evaluate(catalog, query)` that returns a list of items. This method encapsulates the decision about how to handle things.

EXERCISE 77 Evaluate.

> **Should the core of `evaluate()`'s implementation be**
>
> **(a)** `catalog.itemsMatching(query)`
>
> **(b)** `query.matchesIn(catalog)`
>
> **(c)** `process(catalog.data, query.data)` **(that is, this module uses information from each to decide what to do)**
>
> **Argue for and against each choice, and suggest others if you can.**
>
> ■ *See Appendix A for solutions.*

Path 1: Catalog.itemsMatching(query)

We'll work with option (a) for now. For our first cut, we'll start with a Catalog and just use strings for queries and items. Here's a test:

```
Catalog catalog;
public void setUp() {
    catalog = new Catalog();
    catalog.add("Hammer - 10 lb");
    catalog.add("shirt - XL - blue");
    catalog.add("shirt - L - green");
    catalog.add("Halloween candle - orange");
    catalog.add("Halloween candy - gum");
}

public void testSimpleQuery() {
    List result = catalog.itemsMatching("shirt");
    AssertEquals(2, list.size());
}
```

EXERCISE 78   Catalog.

> Write a simple Catalog class with the two implied methods.

EXERCISE 79   Query.

> Extract the current query string into a Query class.

Your Catalog class probably has a line something like

```
if (item.indexOf(query) != -1)
```

Modify this to

```
if (item.indexOf(query.toString()) != -1)
```

as being the least change.

EXERCISE 80   Trading Off Smells.

> Explain how this adds a small case of Feature Envy or Inappropriate Intimacy in the process of cleaning up a little Primitive Obsession.

■ See Appendix A for solutions.

EXERCISE 81   Move to Query.

> *Extract Method* on `item.contains(query.toString())`, then
> *Move Method* to put the matching behavior on the query.
> (In the end, you'll call `query.matches(item)`.)

We'd like to expand our queries to support more complex queries. "Halloween OR shirt" should find several items. In this
exercise, we won't worry about parsing; instead, assume our queries will be composites like that shown in Figure 15.1. We'll call
the top node in the figure an OrQuery, and the others will be
called StringQuery. Both of these will be subclasses of Query.

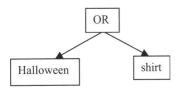

FIGURE 15.1   A Query in the Form of a Composite

EXERCISE 82   StringQuery and Query.

> *Extract Superclass* (or subclass, depending how you look at
> it:), so StringQuery becomes a subclass of Query.

Sometimes you'll hear people speaking of a refactoring *making
room* for new code. This is an example of that: We're making
room for an OrQuery subclass. You could come at it the other
way—introducing the OrQuery and then removing the duplication.

EXERCISE 83   OrQuery.

> **Create an OrQuery class that meets this test:**
>
> ```
> Query query = new OrQuery (
>    new StringQuery("shirt"),
>    new StringQuery("Halloween"));
> list = catalog.itemsMatching(query);
> assertEquals(4, list.size());
> ```

One way to think of this approach is as an example of the Strategy pattern. The catalog is the context, and the different queries
all implement different algorithms for matching. (You might

also detect a Composite pattern in the way the queries are constructed.)

EXERCISE 84   Performance. (Challenging).

> Suppose a profile showed that our queries are too slow. Suppose further that we find our queries are used thousands of times per day in a batch, while additions are done only once per day. We also find that any given word is unlikely to appear in more than a small fraction of the items.
>
> What ways can you suggest to speed up performance?

■ *See Appendix A for solutions.*

PERFORMANCE

We want our systems to have good performance, good response time, and so on, so we sometimes worry about performance of our code. It's a reasonable concern; some refactorings can slow down the system by introducing more objects, more method calls, and and the like.

Other factors counteract this:

- Most untuned code has only a few hot spots where performance matters; we can tune them later.

- A clean design can open the way for deep understanding that makes huge improvements possible.

- It's easier to tune a clean design.

When there are performance worries, there are several ways out:

- Do a thought experiment to see a path toward a performance boost. (For example, we may have linear-search collection, but know that we can index it for higher performance if it turns out we need to.)

- Look for an existence proof that there's a faster way.

- Try a spike—pull out the essential algorithm and play with it separately.

Once we know there is a way to speed up, we have an ace in the hole; we needn't feel compelled to implement it until it's required.

Path 2: Query.matchesIn(catalog)

To explore another way of doing things, we'll start over with the same `setup()` routine, but a different test:

```
Query query = new Query("shirt");
List list = query.matchesIn(catalog);
AssertEquals(2, list.size());
```

EXERCISE 85   A Different Test.

> Implement Catalog and Query for this test. (You'll probably loop over items and call `query.matches(item)` somewhere inside.)

EXERCISE 86   StringQuery and Query Again.

> Refactor StringQuery to be a subclass of Query (as before).

EXERCISE 87   OrQuery Again.

> Implement OrQuery. It should use `matchesIn(catalog)` on each of its subqueries.

You probably found that List wasn't the most convenient type; you'd really prefer a Set (so the OrQuery doesn't produce duplicates). You can change the List types to Sets, but you might also take this as a warning: Perhaps the result wants to be its own object, or perhaps the result of a query is another catalog.

EXERCISE 88   Items versus Sets. (Challenging).

> At some level, this seems more complicated than the earlier implementation. I think it's because the earlier one compared individual items, and this one deals in sets.
>
> A. With this scheme, what sort of queries will go to the catalog?

EXERCISE 88   Items versus Sets. (Challenging). (Continued)

> B. What opportunities are there for performance improvement?
>
> C. Describe this version as an implementation of the Interpreter pattern.

■ *See Appendix A for solutions.*

The first optimization exposed information about the query (words to filter by) to the catalog. The second optimization exposed information about the catalog (sets of items) to the query.

Path 3: Process(catalog.data, query.data)

In the first path, we passed the query to the catalog. In the second path, we passed the catalog to the query. Each of these two ways couples the classes to each other: One must know about the other. A third approach might be to let `Interrogator.evaluate()` take some information from the catalog and combine it with some information from the query, so that only `Interrogator.evaluate()` knows both classes.

EXERCISE 89   FilterEnumerator. (Challenging).

> A. Make Catalog provide an enumerator of its items. Make Query determine whether an item is acceptable. (Both classes know items, but neither knows the other.) Create a FilterEnumerator class: It's an enumerator that takes another enumerator and a query and returns only those items that match the query. Interrogator will set up the objects and use the new enumerator.

EXERCISE 89   FilterEnumerator. (Challenging). (Continued)

> **B. This is an example of a pattern. Which one?**
>
>
> **C. What are the performance implications?**

> ■ *See Appendix A for solutions.*

EXERCISE 90   Other Approaches.

> **Are there other approaches that keep Query and Catalog from knowing about each other?**

Conclusion

We started with two classes that needed to collaborate and looked at three approaches to their core interaction. I don't have a general rule to tell which approach is better. Note that they pointed toward different systems in the end. Choosing the balance of responsibility between objects is still an art.

PLANNING GAME SIMULATOR

We have a GUI program we'd like to clean up. It's a simple simulation of XP's planning game, shown in Figure 16.1. The customer can create new cards, split existing cards, delete old cards, and get a simple analysis of the plan. The programmer can put a cost estimate on a card and update the velocity estimate. In addition, anyone can type on a card or move it around by dragging its border. Notice also that there is summary information on the bottom of the screen, updated after each action.

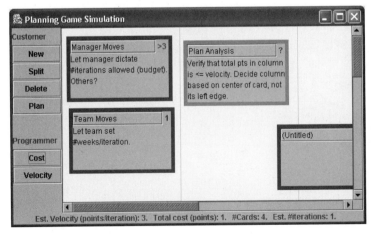

FIGURE 16.1   Simulation of XP's Planning Game

The code for this program is built around three classes: Table (the overall application, including the buttons), Background (where cards are put), and Card (representing an index card).

Part 1: Original Code

Code (Online at *www.xp123.com/rwb*)

Table.java

```java
import java.awt.*;
import java.awt.event.*;
import javax.swing.*;
import javax.swing.event.*;
import javax.swing.text.JTextComponent;

public class Table extends JFrame {
    public static void main(String[] args)
    {
        new Table();
    }

    private JComponent body;
    private Card selection;
    private JLabel summary;
    int velocity = 1;
    int budget = 4;
    JTabbedPane tabs;

    public Table()
    {
        super("Planning Game Simulation");
        JComponent buttons = makeButtons();
        this.getContentPane().add(buttons, "West");

        body = new Background(1000, 1000, 190);
        body.addContainerListener(new ContainerListener() {
            // Listen for container changes so we know when
            // to update selection highlight
            public void componentAdded(ContainerEvent e)
            {
                resetSelection();
            }

            public void componentRemoved(ContainerEvent e)
            {
                resetSelection();
            }

            private void resetSelection()
            {
                if (selection != null)
                    selection.setBorder(
                        BorderFactory.createLineBorder(Color.blue, 6));

                if (body.getComponentCount() == 0) {
```

```
                selection = null;
            } else {
                selection = (Card) body.getComponent(0);
                selection.setBorder(
                    BorderFactory.createLineBorder(Color.red, 6));
            }
        }
    });
    JScrollPane scroll = new JScrollPane(body);
    scroll.setPreferredSize(new Dimension(100, 100));
    this.getContentPane().add(scroll, "Center");

    summary = new JLabel("", SwingConstants.CENTER);
    summary.setText(summary());
    this.getContentPane().add(summary, "South");

    this.pack();
    this.setSize(800, 600);
    this.show();
}

private JComponent makeButtons()
{
    JPanel panel = new JPanel(new GridLayout(0, 1));

    panel.add(new JLabel("Customer"));
    makeCustomerButtons(panel);

    panel.add(new JLabel(" "));

    panel.add(new JLabel("Programmer"));
    makeProgrammerButtons(panel);

    JPanel outer = new JPanel(new BorderLayout());
    outer.add(panel, "North");
    outer.add(new JLabel(""), "Center");
    return outer;
}

private void makeCustomerButtons(JPanel panel)
{
    JButton button;
    button = new JButton("New");
    panel.add(button);
    button.addActionListener(new ActionListener() {
        public void actionPerformed(ActionEvent e)
        {
            Card card = new Card();
            body.add(card, 0);
            selection = card;
            updateCost();
```

```
                repaint();
            }
        });

        button = new JButton("Split");
        panel.add(button);
        button.addActionListener(new ActionListener() {
            public void actionPerformed(ActionEvent e)
            {
                if (selection == null) return;
                Card card = new Card(selection);
                body.add(card, 0);
                selection = card;
                updateCost();
                body.repaint();
            }
        });

        button = new JButton("Delete");
        panel.add(button);
        button.addActionListener(new ActionListener() {
            public void actionPerformed(ActionEvent e)
            {
                if (body.getComponentCount() == 0) return;

                body.remove(0);
                selection = null;
                if (body.getComponentCount() != 0)
                    selection = (Card) body.getComponent(0);
                updateCost();
                body.repaint();
            }
        });


        button = new JButton("Plan");
        panel.add(button);
        button.addActionListener(new ActionListener() {
            public void actionPerformed(ActionEvent e)
            {
                StringBuffer report = new StringBuffer();
                // Check for cards that need est. or splitting
        for (int i = 0; i < body.getComponentCount(); i++) {
                    Card card = (Card) body.getComponent(i);
                    if (card.needsEstimate())
                        report.append(
"Needs estimate: " + card.title() + "\n");
                    else if (card.needsSplit())
                        report.append(
"Needs to be split: " + card.title() + "\n");
                }
```

```
                if (report.length() == 0)
                    JOptionPane.showMessageDialog(
                        body,
                        "Plan OK; no cards need estimates or splitting",
                        "Issues in plan",
                        JOptionPane.OK_OPTION);
                else
                    JOptionPane.showMessageDialog(
                      body, report.toString(),
                      "Issues in plan", JOptionPane.OK_OPTION);
            }
    });
}

private void makeProgrammerButtons(JPanel panel)
{
    JButton button;

    button = new JButton("Cost");
    panel.add(button);
    button.addActionListener(new ActionListener() {
        public void actionPerformed(ActionEvent e)
        {
            if (selection == null) return;
            selection.rotateCost();
            updateCost();
        }
    });

    button = new JButton("Velocity");
    panel.add(button);
    button.addActionListener(new ActionListener() {
        public void actionPerformed(ActionEvent e)
        {
            velocity++;
            if (velocity >= 10) velocity = 1;
            updateCost();

        }
    });
}

private void updateCost()
{
    summary.setText(summary());
}

private String summary()
{
    StringBuffer result = new StringBuffer();
```

```
        result.append(
           "Est. Velocity (points/iteration): " + velocity + ".    ");
        result.append("Total cost (points): " + cost() + ".    ");
        result.append("#Cards: " + body.getComponentCount() + ".    ");
        result.append(
           "Est. #iterations: "
           + (cost() + velocity - 1)/ velocity + ".    ");
        return result.toString();
    }


    // Total cost of the set of cards
    private int cost()
    {
        int total = 0;
        for (int i = 0; i < body.getComponentCount(); i++) {
            Card card = (Card) body.getComponent(i);
            total += card.cost();
        }
        return total;
    }
}
```

Background.java

```java
import java.awt.*;
import javax.swing.*;

public class Background extends JLayeredPane {
    int lineDistance;

    public Background(int width, int height, int lineDistance)
    {
        super();
        setPreferredSize(new Dimension(width, height));
        this.lineDistance = lineDistance;

        setOpaque(true);
        setBackground(Color.yellow);
        setForeground(Color.orange);
    }

    public void paintComponent(Graphics g) {
        super.paintComponent(g);
        int height = getHeight();
        for (int i = 0; i < this.getWidth(); i+= lineDistance)
            g.drawLine(i, 0, i, height);
    }
}
```

Card.java

```java
import java.awt.*;
import java.awt.event.*;
import javax.swing.*;
import javax.swing.border.*;

public class Card extends JPanel {
    static int cards = 0;

    final static int scale = 34;           // card size factor
    final static int height = 3 * scale;   // 3x5
    final static int width = 5 * scale;

    final static int rollover = 12; // New cards go in difft. pos'ns
    final static int offset = scale;// How far apart to put new cards

    JTextField title;
    JTextArea body;
    JLabel costLabel;
    int cost;

    public Card()
    {
        this("(Untitled)", "");
    }

    public Card(Card from)
    {
        this(from.title.getText(), from.body.getText());
    }

    private Card(String titleText, String bodyText)
    {
        super();
        setBorder(BorderFactory.createLineBorder(Color.blue, 6));
        cards++;

        setLayout(new BorderLayout());
        JPanel top = new JPanel(new BorderLayout());

        title = new JTextField(titleText);
        title.setBackground(Color.pink);
        title.addFocusListener(new FocusAdapter() {
            public void focusGained(FocusEvent e)
            {
                moveToFront();
            }
        });

        top.add(title, "Center");
        costLabel = new JLabel(" ? ");
```

```
        cost = 0;
        top.add(costLabel, "East");
        add(top, "North");

        body = new JTextArea(bodyText);
        body.setLineWrap(true);
        body.setWrapStyleWord(true);
        body.setBackground(Color.pink);
        body.addFocusListener(new FocusAdapter() {
            public void focusGained(FocusEvent e)
            {
                moveToFront();
            }
        });

        add(body, "Center");

        setLocation(
            (cards % rollover) * offset,
            (cards % rollover) * offset);
        setSize(width, height);

        // Turn on mouse events so we can detect being dragged
        enableEvents(
            AWTEvent.MOUSE_EVENT_MASK
            | AWTEvent.MOUSE_MOTION_EVENT_MASK);
    }

    private void moveToFront()
    {
        JLayeredPane background = (JLayeredPane) this.getParent();
        background.moveToFront(this);
    }

    private int lastx, lasty;

    public void processMouseEvent(MouseEvent e)
    {
        if (e.getID() == MouseEvent.MOUSE_PRESSED) {
            lastx = e.getX();
            lasty = e.getY();
            moveToFront();
        } else
            super.processMouseEvent(e);
    }

    public void processMouseMotionEvent(MouseEvent e)
    {
        if (e.getID() == MouseEvent.MOUSE_DRAGGED) {
            Point here = getLocation();
            setLocation((int) (here.getX() + e.getX() - lastx),
```

```java
                        (int) (here.getY() + e.getY() - lasty));
        } else
            super.processMouseMotionEvent(e);
    }

    public void rotateCost()
    {
        String label = costLabel.getText();
        if (label.equals(" ? ")) {
            costLabel.setText(" 1 ");
            cost = 1;
        } else if (label.equals(" 1 ")) {
            costLabel.setText(" 2 ");
            cost = 2;
        } else if (label.equals(" 2 ")) {
            costLabel.setText(" 3 ");
            cost = 3;
        } else if (label.equals(" 3 ")) {
            costLabel.setText(" >3 ");
            cost = 0;
        } else if (label.equals(" >3 ")) {
            costLabel.setText(" ? ");
            cost = 0;
        } else {  // shouldn't happen
            costLabel.setText(" ? ");
            cost = 0;
        }
    }

    public int cost()
    {
        return cost;
    }

    public String title()
    {
        return title.getText();
    }

    public boolean needsSplit()
    {
        return costLabel.getText().equals(" >3 ");
    }

    public boolean needsEstimate()
    {
        return costLabel.getText().equals(" ? ");
    }
}
```

Challenges

EXERCISE 91   Smells. (Challenging).

> **A. What smells do you sense in this code? Use the list in the Fowler's *Refactoring* catalog for inspiration; you'll probably find other things as well.**
>
> **B. What strategy (order of refactorings) would you use to improve the code?**
>
> ■ *See Appendix A for solutions.*

EXERCISE 92   Tests. (Challenging).

> **What about tests? The author of this code claimed, "It's basically all GUI, so I couldn't test it." Identify two or three strategies by which we could test this code, with little alteration to the current structure.**
>
> ■ *See Appendix A for solutions.*

EXERCISE 93   Write Tests.

> **Write at least one test for each class, using the simplest strategy you identified.**
>
> ■ *See Appendix A for solutions.*

When faced with a moderately big refactoring task like this, I like to start easy by first fixing smells like Poor Name or Long Method. When code has many things that can be improved, it can be helpful to work with it on its own terms for a while before trying dramatic improvements.

EXERCISE 94 Dead Code.

There is unused code in the Table class (in the form of unreferenced variables). Remove the dead code.

■ *See Appendix A for solutions.*

EXERCISE 95 From Table to PlanningGame.

The class name Table stinks as the name for the top-level class. (What table?!?) Even Main would be a better class name; it wouldn't communicate much, but at least it wouldn't *mis*communicate. Let's try PlanningGame as the name for this class: Rename the class appropriately.

EXERCISE 96 Anonymous Inner Classes.

The PlanningGame class has a number of places that use an anonymous inner class to set up event listeners. (Anonymous inner classes are the ones where the routines are defined in the middle of code; you can spot them by seeing }); somewhere.)

A. *Convert Anonymous Inner Class to Inner Class* by extracting each anonymous inner class to its own inner class.

B. Would they be even better as standalone classes?

■ *See Appendix A for solutions.*

EXERCISE 97   Magic Numbers.

> There are many *magic numbers* floating around. (Some of them might be more accurately called *magic colors*.) Extract each to the top of the class as a final static variable. (Focus on numbers and colors; we'll deal with strings later.)
>
> ■ *See Appendix A for solutions.*

Part 2: Redistributing Features

The story so far: We have a planning game simulator built around three classes—PlanningGame (managing the controls and the background), Background (a playing surface), and Card (for the index cards). We identified a number of places that could be improved, created a few simple tests, and did some simple refactorings. The starting-point code for this part is available at *www.xp123.com/rwb/*.

There were several places in PlanningGame (formerly Table) that accessed fields inside Background. This is a case of Feature Envy: A class spends time manipulating data that is somebody else's responsibility. The cure is to move data and methods around.

EXERCISE 98   Test the Buttons.

> Before we move features around, we want to make sure our tests will warn us if we've done so incorrectly. My tests so far called only publicly available methods, and this didn't include the ability to simulate button clicks. If your tests don't have this ability, add it. (You can expose the buttons one by one, or you might find a more generic approach; once you have a button, you can call doClick() to make it do its thing.)
>
> ■ *See Appendix A for solutions.*

Notice how the Plan button causes trouble: It wants to create a dialog, which is a pain to test programmatically. I'll just leave it for now and be extra careful when working on it. (This is one of those places where you want to refactor to enable you to create a test, but you want a test to help you to refactor safely.)

EXERCISE 99   Move Features to Background.

- **Extract the "string computation" part of the Plan button and move it to Background. (You may have to test it manually, but you should be able to automate a test after the refactoring.)**

- **Move** cost() **to Background.**

- **Create a** count() **method on Background that looks at** getComponentCount()**; adjust the callers.**

- **Create a** top() **method on Background that returns** getComponent(0) **and adjust the callers. (I'd try returning something of type Card for now because the callers all want to cast it anyway.)**

The latter two changes are more in the spirit of improving communication than decoupling.

EXERCISE 100   Move Features to Card.

The Card doesn't know its own selection status. Change that by pulling over the code for a new method setSelected(boolean)**. I had expected to need a method** isSelected()**, but nobody looks at the selection status!**

I'm not fully happy with the selection handling, nor with the fact that the Card knows about its background. But I'm not quite sure how to handle it, and there is still a lot of duplication around the cost in a Card and the button-making in Planning-Game. Since I have ideas for those, I'll tackle them next.

EXERCISE 101   Clean up Cost.

- **Get rid of those annoying spaces surrounding each label. (It's pretty clear they're just for padding.)**

- **Extract a Cost class. Adjust the test classes.**

■ *See Appendix A for solutions.*

Pulling this class out made me wonder where Card.needsEstimate() and Card.needsSplit() are called. Each is called by Background.planAnalysis() and the tests. But planAnalysis() is asking the Card for those checks; why not let the Card compute its own analysis? (Later, there might be other analyses not at card level, but we'll let that day take care of itself.) So eliminate this Feature Envy by putting a `planAnalysis()` method on Card. This is a problem I hadn't noticed earlier, but the refactoring made it clear.

Five Whys

While we're looking at `planAnalysis()`, notice the last argument of `JOptionPane.showMessageDialog()`. In looking over this exercise, my colleague Edmund Schweppe pointed out that OK_OPTION is not the right constant to pass to that method. That argument is intended to tell whether the message is a warning, informational, etc.; if we talk to our customer, we find out that it should be a warning (if there are any problems) or informational (otherwise). It's not unusual to find a bug during refactoring.

Lean manufacturing has the notion of asking why five times to get at the root causes of problems. The outermost symptom is that it always shows the stop sign—is that really what the user wants? One level back, we see that the wrong constant has been used. But why wasn't it detected? One reason is that we don't have any tests for dialog types. (Yes, they're a pain to test.) Note also how the code was formatted: one very long line, with the wrong constant at the far right end. In my editor, this means I would never have a chance to see the constant unless I explicitly went to the end of the line. (Personal resolution: Update my personal coding style to format one argument per line on long lines.)

Why was it written wrong in the first place? One reason is that I didn't have documentation at hand; I relied on the editor to suggest constants and grabbed one that sounded right. (Personal resolution: Get a new Java Foundation Classes manual and don't rely on memory so much.) In this case, I was coding solo—my partner could easily have been looking up the arguments while I was typing.

And why is it possible to make this kind of error? Partly, it's a result of a decision the library designers made: to use only integer constants for all the option types and message types. The library designers could have created separate classes for these options (as a sort of enumeration); or they could have used non-overlapping values or different methods for the different message types. (Personal resolution: Watch out for primitive obsession in my own code, even if I can't do anything about the library's.)

Even a small mistake has the seeds of many lessons.

Removing Duplication, Selection Troubles, and a Few Burrs

So where are we?

- Cost—I'm reasonably happy with this class. There are other ways to do it, but I'll take it as fine for now.
- Card—I'm still not thrilled about the cards/rollover stuff, but I'll leave it. Selection could be improved—should the card notify its focus listeners when it's clicked? This would remove its dependency on Background.
- Background—Other than changing Card and selection, I'm happy with it.
- PlanningGame—There's still duplication in the setup. Colleague Ron Crocker pointed out that we could let `makeCustomerButtons()` and `makeProgrammerButtons()` take the responsibility for putting in the proper label. But the whole handling of containers and selection remains troublesome. And we're still calling `updateCost()` in a bunch of places.

EXERCISE 102   Button Creation.

> **Clean up button creation in PlanningGame.**
>
> - **Move the labels into the "make" routines.**
>
> - **Eliminate the duplication in constructing buttons.**
>
> ■ *See Appendix A for solutions.*

I've been trying to understand why the selection handling bothers me so much. I think it's based on the responsibilities of the classes: I want the planning game screen to be responsible for holding the buttons, the Background, and the summary. Currently, the planning game screen also tracks the selection because that's what the action listeners work with. But I think instead we should make the Background track all selections; some of the action listener work belongs there too.

This change is a bit tentative, so I will certainly *checkpoint* my code so that I can return to it if I don't like where things end up.

(I think of checkpointing as saving a version for easy recovery without releasing it to the whole team; this may or may not be easy in your environment.)

EXERCISE 103   Move Selection Handling to Background.

- **Make Background hold the selection.**

- **Move appropriate listener behavior over to Background (at least from New, Split, and Delete).**

- **Move the ContainerListener.**

■ *See Appendix A for solutions.*

Updating the cost is done by any button press that might change it. Each command must be careful to include a call to updateCost() after any changes it causes. In the current code, this is done by putting the call in each listener. One way to reduce this duplication is to subclass listeners from a common parent and make the parent responsible for the call.

An alternative would be to introduce listener-style notification; the summary would listen for changes in the underlying Background or velocity and would update itself accordingly. PropertyChangeEvent fits our needs. On Background, the two things we typically monitor are the count and the cost. Rather than be specific about which property has changed, I'll use the standard bean convention that null for a property change means anything might have changed.

This change is a refactoring, but it's into the realm of *large* refactoring (or would be if this program were of a substantial size). I don't feel like my tests will adequately cover it, so I'll introduce new tests to make sure Background sends events. Since this is a relatively big change, checkpoint before you start.

EXERCISE 104   Property Changes.

Transform PlanningGame so cost updates are triggered by property changes from Background rather than from explicit calls.

■ *See Appendix A for solutions.*

The action listeners still have duplication: Several of them need to check whether there are any cards before they do their work. This suggests a change: Why not disable them unless they apply? This is a user interface change, but our user likes the idea.

EXERCISE 105   Enable Buttons.

> **Make buttons enabled only when appropriate. (Test first, of course.)**
>
> ■ *See Appendix A for solutions.*

Look back at Card. It still depends on Background. When a card is clicked, it looks at the background and tells the background to move that card to the front. This is an undesirable dependency because Background knows about Card, and Card knows about Background.

EXERCISE 106   Card and Background. (Challenging).

> **Remove Card's dependency on Background.**
>
> • **Make Card send a property notification when it is clicked. (You could make the case for a different notification if you wanted.)**
>
> • **Make Background listen for the new notification.**
>
> • **Remove the ContainerListener aspect of Background. (Since Background now controls the `moveToFront()` call, it already knows when the contents are changing.)**
>
> ■ *See Appendix A for solutions.*

EXERCISE 107   Cleanup.

> **Go through your tests and code one more time, doing any simple cleanup you can.**
>
> ■ *See Appendix A for solutions.*

Now compare your code to the original. Does it communicate better? Is it simpler? Better structured?

Part 3: Pushing the Code Further

Part 3 contains some ideas for pushing the code further, exercises for you to do on your own.

EXERCISE 108   Remaining Smells.

> **What smells remain in your code?**

I've noticed that velocity updates are handled differently than other updates; I still have that *rollover* calculation in Card that I never liked; there are some bits of duplication remaining; and I continue to think a separate model layer would help. In some ways, the current design is near a local maximum—it's becoming reasonable for a design that keeps the model and view together, but we need to go off this hill a little to climb a bigger peak. (The problem is that the code still doesn't communicate something we know: Some parts of this program are affected by its user interface, but others aren't. This is an example of Divergent Change.)

If you're not familiar with the model/view or model/view/controller idea, you may want to do some background reading: See the Observer pattern in Gamma et al.'s *Design Patterns*, the TableModel (or other models) in the Java libraries, or the HotDraw framework (described at *c2.com/cgi?CrcCards* and *www.c2.com/doc/crc/draw.html*).

We might start by creating a Card model. Right away we'll face a decision: Should it contain the model for the title, or should we use the one Java provides in the TextField? If we let the Card have its own model, we'll have to be careful not to cause a notification loop (where the Card notifies the TextField of a change, so it tells the Card, which notifies the TextField, and so on). If we use the Java-provided model, our hookup will be a little trickier.

EXERCISE 109   Separate Model.

A. Make sure to save the old version before you start these changes.

B. Apply *Duplicate Observed Data* to split the Card class into a Card and a CardView. (Note that this is not a trivial refactoring. Don't be surprised if this exercise takes a whole session.)

C. Apply *Duplicate Observed Data* to Background.

- Feel free to make use of the DefaultListModel, which builds in notification.

- You can get very fine-grained notification about list changes, but start by just rebuilding the whole list when told it has changed.

- Note that Card's location and selection status are stored in the view. (Is this the right place?) If you try to regenerate views, you must make sure to track this information.

D. Apply *Duplicate Observed Data* to Plan.

E. Divide the program into two separate packages: one for all the models, the other for views. Let view classes depend on the model classes, but not the other way around. (You may find you need to create separate test classes for models and views.)

F. This was a lot of work. Is it an improvement? What future changes will be easier because we've done this? (If it's not an improvement, restore your old version.)

■ *See Appendix A for solutions.*

EXERCISE 110   An Optimization. (Challenging).

The simplest form of notification looks like this:

```
public void setTitle(String title) {
  this.title = title;
  notify();
}
```

A more sophisticated implementation is:

```
public void setTitle(String title) {
  if (this.title.equals(title)) return;
  this.title = title;
  notify();
}
```

A. When is this a performance optimization?

B. What other purpose does it serve?

■ *See Appendix A for solutions.*

EXERCISE 111   New Features.

Consider new features that might be added. How robust is our implementation in the face of these?

- **New cards should be placed top to bottom and left to right instead of diagonally.**

- **We'd like buttons for the manager or team roles.**

- **All colors and sizes should be made into preferences.**

- **Plan analysis should detect too many points in an iteration.**

- **Save and restore your work via some persistence mechanism.**

- **Allow people on multiple sites to work on the plan at the same time.**

EXERCISE 111   New Features. (Continued)

> What other features might you add?

EXERCISE 112   Test-Driven Development.

> Reimplement this code from scratch, using the test-first approach. Don't look at the old version while you develop the new one. What do you see?

The code for this exercise was not originally written in a test-first way. The experiences of people who do test-driven development indicate that a different design often emerges than the one they expected. Did that happen for you? Is the code better? Are the tests better? How much did the original design influence you?

EXERCISE 113   Lessons from Test-Driven Development.

> Assuming your test-driven code is different from the code you were working with before, could you refactor the old code until it matches the new code? Are there refactorings you would need that are not in any book? What smells could guide you so that you would naturally refactor in that direction? Does this teach you anything about refactoring, or about test-driven development?

17

WHERE TO GO FROM HERE

One of the premises of this book is that refactoring is a skill, one that benefits from practice. Look for opportunities to practice and use this skill.

Books

All the books in the bibliography will repay their study. But, if you haven't yet acquired Martin Fowler's *Refactoring*, you should seriously consider doing so. The exercises in this book touch on perhaps half of the refactorings he catalogs. Tools are getting better at the mechanics of refactoring support, but it will be a long time before they effectively cover every aspect of refactoring that Fowler has cataloged.

Admonitions

Build Refactoring into Your Practice

Knowing how to refactor isn't worth much…unless it's applied. Resolve to make your code lean and clean. On an XP team, this is part of everyday life. But even approaches that are heavily design driven expect programmers to implement the design well.

Build Testing into Your Practice

There's an old adage (as so many are), "If it ain't broke, don't fix it." (How many times has that last simple change caused an unexpected bug?) In programming, the downside of applying this adage is that the code just gets uglier and uglier.

Refactoring is willing to go against this rule through two mechanisms: safe refactorings and a supply of tests to verify that the transformations have been done correctly. Don't neglect your tests.

Get Help from Others

Get other people's opinions about your code, whether through pair programming, design/code reviews, or simply bugging your neighbor. One of the things that really got hammered home to me in writing this book is that almost any code can be improved (and sometimes we get to take advantage of the whole Internet's worth of help!).

Exercises to Try

Smell Scavenger Hunt/Smell of the Week

Pick a smell and find and eliminate as many occurrences of it as you can. Every week, search for a new smell.

Re-Refactor

Pick a good-sized piece of code (either your own or one of the larger examples in the back of this book would work). Each day, start from the initial version and refactor as far as you can in 10 minutes.

Do you sense the same things each day? Do you get farther?

Just Refactor

Pick or develop a project. Spend 10 minutes refactoring. (Each day, start where you left off the day before.)

Inhale/Exhale

Find code demonstrating some smell. Apply a refactoring that addresses it. Then apply the refactoring that reverses the first refactoring. Repeat this twice more. This will give you a sense of what it's like to put a problem into code as well as take one out.

Defactoring/Malfactoring

Defactoring and *malfactoring* are names I use for malicious refactoring: *worsening* the design of existing code. Take some code and refactor it to make it as smelly as possible. (It's harder than it sounds.)

In addition to providing practice at refactoring, this may also help you realize when you're unintentionally malfactoring during development.

Be sure to restore the original after you've had your fun.

Refactoring Kata

A kata is a martial arts exercise that you repeat every day, both for practice and to help get into the rhythm of the art. (A traditional series might be a defense against four opponents.) Develop a kata for refactoring: a program where you'll apply a fixed series of refactorings. Pick a series of smells and refactorings that you see or use often; for me, that might include some Primitive Obsession, some Long Methods, some observed data to duplicate (*Duplicate Observed Data*), and some responsibilities to rebalance.

This will give you a chance to hone your editing skills and enhance your understanding of your environment, as well as to practice smelling and refactoring.

Web Sites

The following Web sites are useful resources:

- *groups.yahoo.com/group/refactoring*. A group for discussing refactoring.
- *groups.yahoo.com/group/extremeprogramming*. A group for discussing XP. There's a lot of discussion unrelated to refactoring, but refactoring is one of the key practices in XP.
- *www.refactoring.com*. Martin Fowler's site, associated with *Refactoring*. He has most of that book's catalog online, along with contributions from others.
- *www.industriallogic.com*. Joshua Kerievsky's corporate site. He's working on a book, *Refactoring to Patterns,* and has interesting articles and games as well.
- *www.xp123.com/rwb*. In general, my site is focused on XP, and the rwb area is devoted to this book. You'll find source code for the larger examples, refactoring-related articles, and pointers to refactoring challenges others have proposed.

SECTION 4

APPENDIXES

APPENDIX A
ANSWERS TO SELECTED QUESTIONS

Chapter 2. The Refactoring Cycle

EXERCISE 1. Small Steps (page 15)

Most refactorings reflect this attitude (safety even in mid-refactoring). Consider our *Encapsulate Field* example. Even this simple program compiled three times. Or look at *Extract Method*: rather than simply cutting the old code and moving it, Fowler's catalog suggests *copying* the code and adjusting it before deleting the old version.

EXERCISE 2. Simple Design (page 15)

A.

1. Passes all tests. "If it doesn't have to work, I can give it to you right now."
2. Communicates. This makes an appeal to our intuition about future readers of our code (including ourselves).
3. No duplication. Duplicate code is asking for trouble; it's too vulnerable to changes in one place but not in the other.
4. Fewest classes and methods. All things being equal, we prefer *smaller* code.

B. For me, the bottom line is that there's an appeal to the code reader's ability to understand; we'll tolerate duplication to achieve better understanding.

Robert Wenner (personal communication) notes that Java Native Interface (JNI) code, linking Java to C, will have duplication between methods, but each method is just different enough to make it difficult to pursue. Each method has to deal with different arguments and different return values for each function it accesses.

Test code will sometimes have duplication for communication reasons. For example, it may be easier to repeat an expected value rather than to assign it to a variable and use the variable. That way, when you read the code, you know exactly what it was looking for, and you don't have to review code to find the variable and make sure nothing else changed it along the way.

Chapter 3. Measured Smells

EXERCISE 3. Comments (page 19)

B. Can everything important about the code be communicated using the code alone? Or do comments have a place?

Code can usually communicate the *how* of something fairly well; it's not always able to communicate the *why* as well; and it's almost impossible to communicate the *why not*.

When code becomes published for others, some people find it important to include JavaDoc comments to provide extra explanation.

EXERCISE 4. Long Method (page 21)

A.

```
Block 1: out.println("FACTORY REPORT\n");
Block 2: From there until out.print ("Robot");
Block 3: From out.print ("Robot"); through write("\n");
Block 4: out.println("======\n");
```

You might have chosen a slightly different set of blocks.

B.

```
public static void report (
  PrintStream out, List machines, Robot robot) {
    reportHeader(out);
    reportMachines(out, machines);
    reportRobot(out, robot);
    reportFooter(out);
}
```

We wouldn't stop here, but this would be a good first step. (We could either move toward a Report class or toward putting report() methods on the Machine and Robot classes.)

C. Does it make sense to extract a one-line method? Yes, if it communicates better.

EXERCISE 5. Large Class (page 26)

A. It's doing a lot of things; some are inherited, but it seems to have a variety of responsibilities.

B. Go through the methods listed, and categorize them into 5 to 10 major areas of responsibility.

My list is as follows (yours will vary):

Columns Editing Rendering Model Selection

Appearance Notification Other

C. It might be possible to generalize addresses so there wouldn't be so much need to have symmetrical row and column functions. It's possible to pull out helper classes that would own some corner of the responsibility. Some of the methods appear simply to consult the table or column model for their answer. The appearance properties could be managed separately or through a simpler interface.

D. I'm not a Smalltalk expert, but I think a few things contribute to the difference:

- Smalltalk's dynamic typing lets generic methods be defined more easily.
- Smalltalk has been around longer, and more methods have worked their way in.
- Smalltalk's interpreted (and more open) environment has encouraged more experimentation.

EXERCISE 6. Long Parameter List (page 31)

A. `x/y/width/height` sounds like a Rectangle object.

`value/extent` sounds like a range. (Notice that the limit parameters use `min` and `max` rather than a second range; the whole thing might be cleaner if there were a separate Range class.)

`x1/y1/x2/y2` sounds like another Rectangle.

B. In some ways, it's a reflection of an attempt to make a class more generic—pass in everything it could work with. Things like graphics tend to want to be stateless, and using lots of parameters can help them do that.

C. There are many occurrences of row/column together; that makes me wonder if the object would be simplified using some sort of locator instead. It would probably simplify selection, and it might address challenges such as cells that span two rows.

EXERCISE 7. Smells and Refactorings (page 32)

A. Comments

B. Large Class

C. Long Method

D. Long Parameter List

B	*Duplicate Observed Data*
B	*Extract Class*
B	*Extract Interface*
A or *C*	*Extract Method*
B	*Extract Subclass*
A	*Introduce Assertion*
D	*Introduce Parameter Object*
D	*Preserve Whole Object*
A	*Rename Method*
D	*Replace Parameter with Method*

EXERCISE 8. Triggers (page 33)

A. Which do you see or create most? Everybody's list will be different. Long Method and (Unhelpful) Comment are the two I see most. Of those, Long Method is probably the one I self-inflict the most.

B. For these measured smells, you can give yourself a cutoff number that tells you to review what you're doing. For example, I check twice if a method exceeds about seven lines, and I question any comments in the body of a method. Define your own triggers.

Interlude 1. Smells and Refactorings

I1-2. Refactorings that Fix the Most Smells (page 35)

Move Method, Extract Class, Move Field, and *Extract Method*

I1-3. Refactorings Not Mentioned (page 35)

It's a long list. Some are just code manipulation; it's not that either way smells, but rather the refactoring provides a safe way to move between two valid alternatives. Others are a bit specialized (especially the "big" refactorings). Others are used as steps in applying another refactoring; the smell for the other refactoring triggers this one.

I1-4. Other Smells (page 35)

Everybody's list will be different. I added these:

- Intertwined Model and UI—*Duplicate Observed Data, Separate Domain from Presentation*
- Cast—*Encapsulate Downcast*
- Unclear Communication—*Remove Assignment to Parameter, Replace Error Code with Exception, Replace Exception with Test, Replace Magic Number with Symbolic Constant, Split Temporary Variable*
- Conditional Logic—*Consolidate Conditional Expression, Consolidate Duplicate Conditional Expression, Introduce Null Object, Replace Error Code with Exception, Replace Exception with Test, Replace Nested Conditional with Guard Clause, Replace Conditional with Polymorphism.*

Chapter 4. Names

EXERCISE 9. Names (page 42)

- `addItem(item)`—embedded type
- `doIt()`—may be OK, may be uncommunicative, depending on context
- `getNodesArrayList()`—embedded type
- `getData()`—uncommunicative (perhaps)
- `makeIt()`—uncommunicative (perhaps)
- `multiplyIntInt()`—embedded type
- `processItem()`—embedded type or uncommunicative
- `sort()`—OK
- `spin()`—OK (depending on the domain)

EXERCISE 10. Critique the Names (page 43)

If there's an area of personal taste, it's probably in names. Don't be surprised if your answers differ.

A. `Clear()` or `erase()` both sound OK (depending on whatever the library or other code uses). `DeleteAll()` seems clunky. `Wash()` might be OK for a pane-of-glass simulation, but it seems strained for this purpose.

B. Push() is traditional; add() is probably OK if that's what everything else in the collection library is using. Insert() seems misleading, since stacks don't put items in the middle. AddToFront() is odd as well; we think of queues having fronts but of stacks as having tops.

C. Cut() implies that the text is saved somewhere for pasting. delete() is probably best; clear() and erase() may be OK, but to my ears they sound like they might apply to the whole document.

D. Equals() is the out-of-the-box Java word. IdenticalTo() might work if equals() is inappropriate for some reason. Matches() could work, but carries a little baggage suggesting it might be a pattern match. Compare() is the worst of the lot; the other terms let us know "returns true if they're equal"; compare() doesn't tell us which way the answer will come out.

EXERCISE 11. XmlEditor (page 44)

A. My choice for the parent class would be Editor.

B. The interface can be called Editor, and the parent of XmlEditor can be called AbstractEditor. (I'd be content to let it evolve; it might happen that the only classes would be an interface Editor and an implementation XmlEditor.)

Chapter 5. Unnecessary Complexity

EXERCISE 12. Today versus Tomorrow (page 47)

FORCES THAT MAKE IT BETTER TO DESIGN FOR ONLY TODAY'S REQUIREMENTS TODAY	FORCES THAT MAKE IT BETTER TO DESIGN FOR TOMORROW'S REQUIREMENTS TODAY
It's cheaper for now to do only today's design.	It may be easier to fully flesh out the class while it's still fresh in our minds today.
We're not committed to requirements evolving in a particular direction (so we don't have to backtrack).	Developing for tomorrow's needs may help us understand today's needs better.
We're not required to maintain tomorrow's code today.	
Code is easier to understand when it does as little as it needs to.	

It all comes down to a bet: on average, will it be cheaper to do only today's design and deal with tomorrow when it comes, or do the generalized designs pay for themselves by being right often enough?

Gordon Bell, one of the great hardware designers, once said, "The cheapest, fastest, and most reliable components of a computer system are those that aren't there." (Quoted in Bentley, *More Programming Pearls,* p. 62.)

Chapter 6. Duplication

EXERCISE 13. Two Libraries (page 55)

A. One strategy:

- Define a new logger whose interface is compatible with the JDK 1.4 logger. It could be a simplified *layer* interface or a class with a compatible interface (that in the future would be a subclass of the JDK 1.4 logger), or it might be a straightforward implementation of the new classes.
- Make the old loggers call the new logger.
- Modify Log and its callers to become like the new logger, so you can delete the Log class.
- Modify Logger to become like the new logger, so you can delete the Logger class too.

There will be a temptation to do this relatively slowly (i.e., for now, use the new logger for new and changed code). Note that this adds to our conceptual burden. You might be able to use automated support to make it easier.

EXERCISE 14. Properties (page 56)

A. Use *Extract Method* to pull out a routine that looks up the property, converts it to an integer, and validates it as positive. (Do this in steps: first, second, and third copies.)

You might determine that it's OK to set monitorTime and departureOffset even if the exception will be thrown. This will reduce the need for temps.

The end result might look like this:

```
checkInterval = getProperty("interval");
monitorTime = getProperty("duration");
departureOffset = getProperty("departure");

if ((monitorTime % checkInterval) != 0)
  throw new MissingPropertiesException(
    "duration % checkInterval");
```

```
if ((departureOffset % checkInterval) != 0)
  throw new MissingPropertiesException(
    "departure % checkInterval");
```

You might then extract a separate method to enforce the % restriction.

EXERCISE 15. Template Example (page 57)

A. Duplication

- The whole thing is two nearly identical copies, one for %CODE% and one for %ALTCODE%. However, one case writes to a string, the other to an output stream.
- The string literal %CODE% and the numeric literal 6 are aspects of the same thing (magic number). Likewise %ALTCODE% and 9.
- The construction of the resulting final string for each part is similar: appending a prefix, body, and suffix.

B. Remove duplication

- *Replace Magic Number with Symbolic Constant* (and with functions)
- Extract Method
- Look into unifying string and input/output (I/O) so we can make the methods even more similar.

C. new String()

- What does it do? The new causes a new string with identical contents to be created. The new string equals() the old but is a different object.
- The intern() method returns a unique instance of the string that will be the same object as all other internalized strings with the same content. (By default, strings are not required to be shared.)
- Does it apply here? No. Since we never compare internalized strings, the new String part is redundant.

EXERCISE 16. Duplicate Observed Data (page 58)

A. The duplication is often not as dramatic as it first appears. Often, the domain object has its own object representation of itself, and the widget ends up holding a string or other display representation.

- The user interface is usually one of the most volatile parts of a program, while the domain classes tend to be modified less often (during development).
- Putting the domain information in the widget ties them together. A domain class should be able to change its value independent of whether the value is displayed on the screen. (See the Observer pattern.)
- Mixing domain and screen classes makes the domain depend on its presentation; this is backwards. It's better to have them separate so the domain classes can be used with an entirely different presentation.

B. The performance can go either way. When they're in one object, the domain class updates its value using widget methods. This is typically slower because it must take into account buffering, screen updating, etc.

On the other hand, the synchronization can become relatively costly. Occasionally you have to find a way to make this notification cheaper. In some situations, splitting the domain class and the widget will let the widget avoid being displayed

EXERCISE 17. Java Libraries (page 59)

A. Examples

- AWT versus Swing: There are two whole widget libraries included.
- Collections versus Vector/HashTable: There are two collection libraries.
- Event listeners: There are many closely related variations.
- Duplicate methods in GUI classes; e.g., `show()` versus `set-Visible()`.
- Others.

B. Why?

- The most common reason seems to be that old chestnut—historical reasons. Sun is understandably reluctant to change published interfaces that many people depend on. Instead of changing things, they add more, even if it overlaps in intent or code.

  Java has a deprecation flag that can be set and is set for some of these duplications. This warns clients that they're depending on the old way of doing things and that there's a better way.

- In something as big as Java's libraries, there are many people working on them, and they don't always coordinate well enough to realize that they've duplicated work.
- Java's libraries are very public (with many books and articles describing them in detail). This means they're subjected to more scrutiny than most efforts. In other words, their duplication may be no worse than others, it's just that they're more visible.

EXERCISE 18. Points (page 59)

A. Both are using points that wrap around the `maxX` and `maxY` values.

B. *Substitute Algorithm* to make both classes calculate wrapping the same way. Then *Extract Class* to pull out a WrappingPoint class.

C. The search for duplication can help you identify these situations. You can create a test that reveals the bug in the bad code. While you fix it, you can drive toward similarity to the good code and then use the refactorings that address duplication to clean up the duplication.

EXERCISE 19. Expression (page 60)

A. You could use Extract Method on the return statements, so `return v1 + v2;` becomes `return value(v1,v2);` and similarly for `*`. This makes the `value()` routines identical, so you can *Pull Up Method* to bring them to the Composite node. (The two-argument routine will still have to be in the subclasses.)

Chapter 7. Conditional Logic

EXERCISE 20. Null Object (page 64)

A. An empty string may not be the right choice for a default value in every context.

B. It's possible that extracting a new class for Bin might give you the needed flexibility.

EXERCISE 21. Conditional Expression (page 66)

A.

```
if ((score <= 700) &&
   ((income < 40000) || (income > 100000)
      || !authorized || (score <= 500)) &&
```

```
  (income  <= 100000))
  reject()
else
  accept();
```

B.

```
boolean hasMidRangeIncome =
  (income >= 40000) && (income <= 100000);
boolean hasHighIncome = (income > 100000);

boolean hasHighScore = (score > 700);
boolean hasMidScore = (score > 500);

if (! (hasHighScore
    || (hasMidRangeIncome && authorized && hasMidRangeScore)
    || hasHighIncome) )
  reject();
else
  accept();
```

C.

```
if (score > 700)
  accept();
else if ((income >= 40000) && (income <= 100000)
    && authorized && (score > 500))
  accept();
else if (income > 100000)
  accept();
else
  reject();
```

D.

```
boolean acceptable(int income, int score, boolean authorized)
{
  if ((score > 700) || (income > 100000))
    return true;

  if ((income >= 40000) && (income <= 100000)
      && authorized && (score > 500))
    return true;

  return false;
}

if (acceptable(income, score, authorized))
  accept();
else
  reject();
```

F.

	HIGH INCOME		MEDIUM INCOME		LOW INCOME	
	AUTH=Y	**AUTH=N**	**AUTH=Y**	**AUTH=N**	**AUTH=Y**	**AUTH=N**
HIGH SCORE	Accept	Accept	Accept	Accept	Accept	Accept
MID SCORE	Accept	Accept	Accept	Reject	Reject	Reject
LOW SCORE	Accept	Accept	Reject	Reject	Reject	Reject

Or, alternatively:

	HIGH INCOME	MEDIUM INCOME	LOW INCOME
HIGH SCORE	Accept	Accept	Accept
MID SCORE	Accept	Accept if authorized	Reject
LOW SCORE	Accept	Reject	Reject

EXERCISE 22. Switch Statement (page 69)

A. If this were all there were to it, you might not bother eliminating the switch. But it would already be very natural to have print() and do() methods on operations to let us eliminate the type field.

EXERCISE 23. Factory Method (page 70)

B. You can argue it either way, but it's starting to get kind of big for an enumeration of integers.

C. What are some advantages to using dynamic class loading?

- The code is simpler (no conditional logic; a single place where class is created).
- The code has fewer direct dependencies (doesn't name the actual driver classes).
- The delivered code can be smaller (it's no longer necessary to deliver the debugging driver class—nothing depends on it directly).
- New driver classes can be dynamically loaded without having to recompile the whole system.

D. What are some disadvantages to this new arrangement?

- Performance is potentially a little worse.
- A simple text scan no longer reveals all the dependencies of the code.
- The configuration is a little trickier; an incorrect name or a bad CLASSPATH can leave the system unable to run.

Interlude 3. Design Patterns

I3-1. Patterns (page 71)

- Abstract Factory: *Replace Constructor with Factory Method* (several times)
- Factory Method: *Replace Constructor with Factory Method*
- Flyweight: *Remove Setting Method, Change Value to Reference*
- Interpreter: *Extract Method* and *Move Method* (from Composite)
- Observer: *Separate Domain from Presentation, Duplicate Observed Data*
- State: *Replace Type Code with State/Strategy*
- Strategy: *Replace Type Code with State/Strategy*
- Template Method: *Form Template Method*

Joshua Kerievsky is working on a book about this subject called *Refactoring to Patterns;* perhaps it will be available by the time you read this.

Chapter 8. Data

EXERCISE 24. Alternative Representations (page 77)

Money (based on U.S. currency, where 100 cents = 1 dollar, and a cent [a penny] is the smallest coin):

- Integer count of cents.
- A pair of integers managed as a *long long*.
- Use a decimal type.
- You may have to track fractions of pennies. (Some money is managed in terms of 1/10 cent.)
- String.

Position (in a list):

- Integer.
- If there's only one position of interest, you might manage *the* list (as seen from outside) via two lists, one containing what comes before the position and the second containing what comes after the position.
- The item at that position.

Range:

- First and last index
- First index and length

Social Security Number (government identification number: "123-45-6789")

- String
- Integer
- Three integers

Telephone number:

- String
- Integer
- Two numbers: area code and local number
- Three numbers: area code, exchange, and last four digits

This only considers U.S. phone numbers; it will be more complicated if you add international phone number support. You also may have to support extensions.

Street Address ("123 E. Main Street"):

- String
- Multiple fields
- Physical coordinates
- Standardized address (standard abbreviations)
- Index in a standard list of addresses

ZIP (postal) code:

- String
- Integer
- Two integers (U.S. postal codes now use ZIP + 4 or 12345-6789)
- Index in a standard list of codes

EXERCISE 25. A Counterargument (page 78)

It depends on what's happening between the screen and the database. If it's truly a form-filling application, to get this field from the screen into that field on the database, we might not use an object-oriented approach. But as more functions are added that concern ZIP codes (validation, computing shipping distances, mapping routes, etc.), we'll expect more benefit from the object-oriented approach.

EXERCISE 26. Iterator (page 78)

When we use the Iterator, the code relies less on the "for" loop approach, so there will be less use of integers as position counters.

EXERCISE 27. Editor (page 78)

```
assertEquals(___, editor.fetch(1));
```

A. Given the interface provided, what string would you expect to use in place of the ___?

"a"

B. Based on the variable name (`firstParendPosition`), what string might you like to use instead? Of what use would this be?

"("

It is sometimes useful to have positions that remember where they are, even if text is inserted in front of them. For example, a programming editor might track the position of each method declaration.

C. The crux of the problem is the use of `int` as a position index. Suggest an alternative approach.

Instead of handing out dead integers, hand out Position objects, but let the editor own them. When text changes, the editor updates the Positions. The holders of the objects aren't aware of that; they just know that they can get one or hand it back to move to a prior position.

D. Relate your solution to the Memento design pattern.

Memento uses an *opaque* object; in this case, the editor may know what's inside, but clients definitely don't. The client can't manipulate the Memento pattern directly, but must hand it back to the main object to use it.

EXERCISE 28. Library Classes (page 80)

- All have public data members.
- All are subclasses of the class Object.
- Most are very stable.
- Most have a well-understood meaning outside of their use in Java (with the exception of GridBagConstraints).
- There may be a lot of them.

EXERCISE 29. Color and Date (page 81)

A. The Color constructor shows three different representations: an RGB (Red/Green/Blue) triple of integers, a single integer holding all the values, or an RGB triple of floats. The color value could be an HSB (Hue/Saturation/Brightness) triple as well.

Date could be stored as a set of values (year, month, day, etc.), as an integer count (seconds or microseconds since some event), or it could even be stored as text.

B. Because clients have no direct access to the fields, they can't change an instance behind that object's back (without going through its methods).

EXERCISE 30. Proper Names (page 81)

A. Client 1 produces a string in first-name-first format; clients 2, 3, and 4 produce a last-name-first string. Put methods on Person for these two variants. You may then be able to *Encapsulate Field*, making the fields private.

B. It will be easier to handle these changes once the duplication is consolidated.

Chapter 9. Inheritance

EXERCISE 31. Collection Classes (page 89)

A. The read-only collections throw an exception, so it's an honest refusal.

B. Java doesn't require explicit declaration of all exceptions, and these are of the type that needn't be declared.

C. One alternative would be to let every collection class come in two flavors: one for read-only and one for not. This would lead to a lot of near-duplicate classes. Refused Bequest seems like the lesser evil.

EXERCISE 33. Swing Libraries (page 91)

A. The interface expresses the essential information about the object and helps decouple clients from the detailed classes. Furthermore, Java supports multiple inheritance of interfaces, but only single inheritance for classes. By keeping the interface separate, classes can add support for the interface, but keep their original hierarchy otherwise.

B. While the framework has only one implementation of the class, it's expected that users of the framework will introduce other classes, and the abstract class forms a handy root for that. If there were no other classes coming, it's conceivable that you might still decide to split out the abstract class just to make the code communicate better.

C. You probably wouldn't start with this structure, but it represents a possible evolutionary path for your code.

Chapter 10. Responsibility

EXERCISE 34. Feature Envy (page 94)

Give Machine and Robot their own `report()` methods.

EXERCISE 35. Walking a List (page 98)

A. The code relies on the fact that machines are maintained as a list.

B. The presence of the list could be a secret of a Machines or Line class.

Exercies 36. Middle Man (page 98)

A. Is a removed middle man an improvement? Not to my eyes—we've reduced the clarity of our code if nothing else. If the event handler is given an ArrayList, it implies a lot more freedom to change it. With the Queue class, we know it's a queue: we can see exactly where the delegate gets touched. Without the Queue class, we have to look across every event handler to be sure that nonqueue operations aren't used.

EXERCISE 37. Cart (page 99)

B. Add `cost()` and `days()` to Purchase.

C. Cart doesn't need access to `item()` or `shipping()` anymore. So hiding the delegate widens the interface as we create methods for related objects, but it may let us narrow the interface because the client no longer needs to navigate.

D. Drop them.

E. It probably doesn't make a whole lot of difference in which order we change these.

EXERCISE 38. Trees in Swing (page 100)

A. TreeModel breaks the class dependency because JTree and DefaultTreeModel both depend on TreeModel, but JTree doesn't depend on DefaultTreeModel.

B. Package dependency still exists because JTree is in the javax.swing package, and it is depending on a class in the javax.swing.tree package. (Think of a package dependency as implying that everything in the package is brought in along with everything it depends on. At the package level, JTree depends both on interfaces and on concrete classes.)

C. There are two approaches we can take to break the package dependency.

One approach would be to move the TreeModel into the package with JTree. This leaves javax.swing.tree dependent on javax.swing, but not vice versa. That's an improvement because, if you implemented your own tree model class, you wouldn't need any of the javax.swing.tree package to be present. It's still troubling, though, in that, if you want to create a tree model that doesn't need a JTree to display it, you'd still have that dependency at the package level.

A second approach would be to pull the TreeModel into its own package (depending on nothing). Let javax.swing depend on the package, and let javax.swing.tree depend on the package, but do not let them depend on each other.

Class loading doesn't actually load one package at a time, so package dependency is something of an intellectual construct. But I find it helpful to consider these dependencies, as they can reveal places where things that *should* be stable rely on things that *change*, rather than vice versa. (See Robert Martin's book, *Agile Software Development: Principles, Patterns, and Practices,* for more on dependency rules.)

D. In a world of abundant disk space, it matters for two reasons: First, extra dependencies reveal places where we haven't worked our way to understanding the minimum our classes need to do. Second, not everything is a desktop system with a huge disk; look at the challenges J2ME has had in getting to a minimum-weight library. For an extra exercise, consider what classes are brought in if you want the minimum to support Object. (Try at both the class and package levels.)

Chapter 11. Accommodating Change

EXERCISE 39. CsvWriter (page 104)

A. One decision is *where* to write; the other decision is *how* to write.

D. Which is better? They're probably not different enough to matter. Either approach could have evolved from a test-driven perspective. It's a bit easier to test the version that produces only a string.

EXERCISE 40. CheckingAccount (page 106)

A. One decision is the relationship between CheckingAccount and Transaction; another decision is the representation for money.

EXERCISE 42. Duplicate Observed Data (page 109)

This might or might not be a problem. The model/view split often arises out of a real need: pressures to change models and views independently. While the hierarchies may start out in parallel, they needn't remain that way. (You might have multiple views for one model and no views for another.)

You may find that generic models emerge. (Think of how TableModel serves as a generic model for many tablelike things.)

EXERCISE 43. Documents (page 110)

A. It affects places all over the class hierarchy.

B. Whether it will be an improvement depends on how it will be used. We don't have enough information to judge.

C. The brief/full and compression/none distinctions will become the *wrapping* types.

Chapter 12. Library Classes

EXERCISE 44. Layers (page 112)

A.

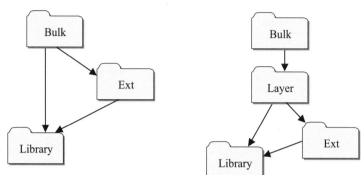

B. In the first case, code depends directly on the library. In the second case, it depends directly on the layer and only indirectly on the library.

C.

- Conceptual Integrity: It depends—a good layer interface can improve the way we think about things.
- Portability: Better; changes will be concentrated in the layer.
- Performance: It can go either way. There's a small cost to going through the layer, but the layer may be able to cache data or otherwise speed up performance.
- Testing: It may be easier to test in the layer, especially if the layer's interface is narrower. It may make it easier to swap in a test implementation as well.

D. Java doesn't have language mechanisms to enforce it. You might have external mechanisms (e.g., a tool that checks references to the layered packages).

EXERCISE 45. Trees (page 113)

A. A foreign method seems easier. Since we already have to modify our node to implement the interface, we can put it there. A local extension might be a new subinterface of MutableTree-Node; this would seem better only if the tree clients could use the userObject without caring about our node type.

EXERCISE 46. String (page 114)

A. Declaring a class `final` prevents creation of a subclass. This makes it impossible to use *Introduce Local Extension*.

B. There may be other reasons, but one reason the String class is `final` has to do with security. In Java, strings are immutable— once set, they cannot be changed. Some security checks rely on this fact. A subclass might subvert immutability. (There may be a performance benefit as well; substring operations can point to part of a string known not to change.)

EXERCISE 47. Filter (page 115)

B. Implements Enumerator.

C. Takes an enumerator (the one to be filtered).

D. Defines the required methods (`hasMoreElements()` and `nextEle-ment()`), and a new method `isValid()` for its subclasses to override.

EXERCISE 48. Diagrams (page 115)

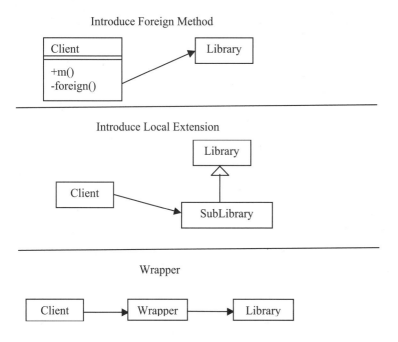

EXERCISE 49. A Missing Function (page 116)

It's probably easiest to introduce a foreign method on one of your classes.

Interlude 4. Gen-A-Refactoring

I4-1. Verbs and Nouns (page 117)

In the table below, put a dash (—) in combinations that don't make sense, a plus sign (+) in those that are in Fowler's catalog, and an asterisk (*) in those that make sense but aren't in the catalog.

	Extract	**Inline**	**Move**	**Rename**	**Pull Up**	**Push Down**	**Hide**	**Expose**
Field	—	—	+	*	+	+	*	*
Method	+	+	+	+	+	+	+	*
Class	+	+	*	*	—	—	*	*
Interface	+	*	*	*	—	—	*	*
Subclass	+	+	—	—	—	—	—	—
Superclass	+	+	—	—	—	—	—	—
Hierarchy	+	*	—	—	—	—	—	—

Some are arguable, especially if you want to consider inner classes.

Chapter 13. A Database Example

EXERCISE 50. Database Smells (page 122)

A. Potential problems?

- There's no indication of what the keys are in each table.
- There is inconsistent use of IDs for keys. (Can two different John Smiths register for classes?)
- Students have no existence apart from their presence in a schedule.
- DaysTimes is not atomic. It can be broken into smaller parts.

A good rule in table design is this: Each row depends on the key, the whole key, and nothing but the key.

B. Fixes?

- Identify keys: Course: Name; Offering: ID; Schedule: Name + OfferingID.

- Give ID fields to Course and Student.
- Extract a Student table.
- Turn each session time into its own row (perhaps in another table).

EXERCISE 51. Duplication (page 135)

A. Duplication:

- Each class loads the database driver (just in case).
- Each class defines a `create()` method (similar but not identical).
- Many `find()` and `update()` methods are similar.
- Test classes have duplicate setups.

Test cases could communicate better. (How about an explanation string on the less obvious asserts?)

Divergent change: classes depend on both the database and the domain.

Course and Offering pretty much consist of public access methods, with little behavior of their own.

We may be missing some collection classes.

B. `Create()` creates the object in memory, and `all()` or `find()` can locate an existing copy. Code manipulates the object in memory and then calls `update()` to write it. There's no general approach to deleting objects.

EXERCISE 52. Application (page 135)

B. It makes sense to create a class to represent tables. It may be easiest to start by making this the superclass, but in the long run we'd probably evolve to having it in a separate part of the hierarchy from our domain objects.

EXERCISE 53. Database Layer (page 136)

A. It would probably be easier to do some cleanup first and define a separable persistence layer.

B. A layer would make it easier to test the domain model and database code separately. A memory-based database would improve the running speed of many tests, because not all tests need the slow-but-safe disk-based database.

C. There's no reason to expose any of JDBC.

EXERCISE 54. Find (page 136)

B. This probably crosses the line into being development.

C. We could put the objects in the map instead of the keys.

EXERCISE 55. Multiple Open Inquiries (page 137)

A. It could potentially affect a lot of code.

B. One approach would be to load only the *keys* of related objects. When a client does a get on the corresponding field, then do a lookup based on the stored key. You could optionally cache the reference.

EXERCISE 56. Counter (page 138)

This can be problematic if there's more than one process or thread simultaneously accessing the database. The usual solution is to introduce transactions. (Some databases may have a simple solution for the special case of a counter, but in general we may need transactions.)

EXERCISE 58. Database Refactorings (page 138)

Look for work by Martin Fowler and Scott Ambler in this area.

EXERCISE 59. Domain Class Independence (page 139)

Ideally, the database classes will depend on the data model rather than vice versa.

Chapter 14. A Simple Game

EXERCISE 60. Smells (page 143)

- The board is represented as a StringBuffer; it could be a new class.
- It might make sense to have a Player class.
- There are a lot of magic numbers.
- There are several complicated if statements.
- There's a lot of duplication—note the winner calculation in particular.
- See also Exercise 61.

EXERCISE 62. Fuse Loops (page 144)

- It's easiest if both loops have the same range.

- It's important that the ith entry of the second loop not depend on anything past the ith entry in the first loop.

Chapter 15. Catalog

EXERCISE 77. Evaluate (page 151)

A. This feels natural to write, but the catalog has to know about the query.

B. The query has to know about the catalog.

C. The catalog and the query needn't know about each other, but they each must expose some of their own information.

EXERCISE 80. Trading off Smells (page 152)

It was Primitive Obsession because our query was originally just a string. You might call it Feature Envy or Inappropriate Intimacy because the `toString()` method is exposing internal details of the query (its string), and its caller makes a decision, instead of the query deciding for itself.

EXERCISE 84. Performance (page 154)

- Since search outnumbers add, anything we do to speed up search at add's expense will speed up the overall system. This suggests that we could process the catalog after the last add, in such a way as to speed up searches.
- The way we've set up the interaction, the catalog has no idea what the search will do. One way to speed up search would be to couple them more. Suppose queries were willing to tell the catalog "one of these words must appear in any item I'd potentially be willing to select." Then we could cache a map of words to candidate items and search many fewer items.

EXERCISE 88. Items versus Sets (page 155)

A. Only StringQueries go to the catalog; others are built out of the results of queries.

B. We definitely want to move to a Set type. Again, the trick will be a good preparation after the adds are done. We could prebuild a map from words (i.e., the StringQuery's query string) to sets of items; this would turn simple queries into a lookup instead of a scan.

C. Interpreter—think of matchesIn() as the evaluation method, and the catalog as the context. The computation "bubbles up" the results of the query.

EXERCISE 89. FilterEnumerator (page 156)

B. It's an example of Decorator (and Iterator, and probably others as well).

C. The biggest problem is that the enumerator implies we have to look at every entry. The other approaches are able to avoid this.

Chapter 16. Planning Game

EXERCISE 91. Smells (page 168)

A. Smells

Long Method

- Several methods in Table are too long, especially with the action code embedded. It's hard to see where layout ends and action begins.
- Card has similar problems. The constructor in particular seems long.

Large Class

- Both Table and Card seem to be doing too much. (There's no separate model, so these classes act as model, view, and controller.)

Duplicated Code

- Code for setting up all the buttons is similar.
- Each action seems to duplicate some of the work in maintaining the selection.
- Both Table and Card set the border color.
- In Card, the title and the text have similar setups.
- String names of costs appear several times.
- Spaces surround each cost name. (Perhaps the label could be designed to have the space.)
- I'm sure I'll find more once I clean some things up.

Divergent Change

- You can't change the GUI and the actions separately; you couldn't run easily without a GUI.

Shotgun Surgery (one change requires touching several areas)

- The highlighting code (the card border) is in two separate objects.

Feature Envy

- Again, highlighting belongs to Card but Table seems to want in on it.
- Cost information is computed in Table, but it does this by pulling apart what's in the Background.
- The summary and the plan report, as well as several of the actions, also pull information out of the Background.

Data Clumps

- The costLabel and the cost variable seem to go together.
- Lastx/lasty, x/y, getX()/getY() deal with paired values.

Primitive Obsession

- Int for x/y
- Int for velocity
- Strings for BorderLayout (there are constants defined)
- Strings for the cost label

Switch Statements

- The rotateCost() method uses an if statement that is practically a switch.

Lazy Class

- The Background is a pretty small class. I could see making some of the setup be the caller's responsibility. I'm not ready to label this a Lazy Class though; the Feature Envy of Table for Background's components makes me expect some methods will move over here.

Speculative Generality/Dead Code

- There are a couple unused variables: budget and tabs.

Temporary Field

- The selection (in Table) has a little of this feel. (Sometimes it's set, sometimes it's null.)

Inappropriate Intimacy

- Table looks into Background's component list.

- Card knows a bit about its Background (it uses this information in `moveToFront()`).

What else?

- The names need some work. *Table* is especially bad. `UpdateCost()` is updating a summary of more than just cost.
- The ContainerListener business seems awkward (as does all of selection).
- Each action calls `updateCost()` to update the summary section. (Could the event model handle this more cleanly?)
- Counting the cards and the rollover count (to set the initial location) is also awkward. Again—how much configuration should be inside a component, and how much outside?
- There's no separate model. At some level, I can accept that—this is trying to be a simple implementation. But we're already to the point where that seems troublesome (e.g., the summary updates).
- There are magic numbers (and colors and strings) in various places.
- The buttons could go into a Box instead of the combination of panels it uses now.

When looking for various smells, we keep returning to the same issues. This is partly the result of the smells not being completely orthogonal, but it's also that the same problem can give off different smells.

B. My planned strategy for fixing this:

- Do trivial things first: fix names, long methods, magic numbers, and such.
- Move things related to Background over to that class.
- See what duplication we can eliminate.
- Straighten out selection. This will involve moving features between classes and might introduce new classes.
- Assess whether cost and velocity should be their own classes.
- See where things are, but I'd expect to split the model out.

EXERCISE 92. Tests (page 168)

From easy (low impact) on up:

- Test the classes as is. For example, you could call rotate-Cost() and verify the resulting cost().
- Develop methods that *walk* the components tree to find particular components. For example, you could find the New button, call its doClick() method, and then verify that the body had one more Card.
- Expose the instance variables of the classes so the tests can more directly access components.
- Restructure the application for better testability. For example, have a separate, easily tested model, along with a thin, *trivial* GUI layer.

EXERCISE 93. Write Tests (page 168)

Using the simplest approach, which was to create objects *as is* and call public methods, the test class tests at least something for each object. This test is in the code in Part 2 of this chapter.

EXERCISE 94. Dead Code (page 169)

Variables budget and tabs are unused.

EXERCISE 96. Anonymous Inner Classes (page 169)

B. You'll often find it helpful to change inner classes to separate classes; it can make it easier to see duplication.

EXERCISE 97. Magic Numbers (page 170)

The result is the starting point for Part 2, the code is online.

EXERCISE 98. Test the Buttons (page 170)

Before we move features around, we want to make sure our tests will warn us if we've done so incorrectly. My tests so far have called only publicly available methods, and this didn't include the ability to simulate button clicks. If your tests don't have this ability, add it. You can expose the buttons one by one, or you might find a more generic approach; then call doClick().

Add the extra tests. I made the buttons have package-level access so the test could get to them. I didn't handle the dialog for the Plan button.

EXERCISE 101. Clean up Cost (page 171)

I made Cost have a list of its possible values, with each value showing its name and cost as well as whether it needs an estimate or to be split.

EXERCISE 102. Button Creation (page 173)

It's easy to extract a method that creates each button and adds it to a panel.

EXERCISE 103. Move Selection Handling to Background (page 174)

I used Encapsulate Fields on the selection in PlanningGame, so the setter and getter were the only things accessing the selection. Then it was easy to Move Field over to Background. In moving the listener over, I left the guard part on the button and made the actions assume they were called appropriately. For the ContainerListener, I made Background become a ContainerListener rather than maintain a separate class. (This could have gone either way.) Finally, I went through and made methods private where I could.

EXERCISE 104. Property Changes (page 174)

This requires PlanningGame to have a listener, but it lets us eliminate the updateCost() calls.

EXERCISE 105. Enable Buttons (page 175)

I added a parameter to makeButton() to tell whether the button was sensitive to the number of cards.

EXERCISE 106. Card and Background (page 175)

This was a little trickier than I expected—there are already other property change notifications when the border is changed. I used a new property name and made Background listen for those notifications.

EXERCISE 107. Cleanup (page 175)

I restructured the resetSelection() handling, reduced some duplication in the actions for creating a new card and splitting a card, and did a few other bits of polishing.

EXERCISE 109. Separate Model (page 177)

F. It's an improvement in my eyes. Now the GUI and the model can change independently.

EXERCISE 110. An Optimization (page 178)

A. The proposed code is faster when the cost of the string comparison is less than the cost of the notification.

B. It can help prevent subtle loops where setting the model notifies a listener, which updates a field, which notifies a listener that updates the model, and so on, in an infinite loop.

APPENDIX B

JAVA REFACTORING TOOLS

Several of the programming environments for Java are adding refactoring support.

TOOL	COMPANY	TYPE	URL
Borland Together	Borland	UML tool with Java and refactoring support	*www.borland.com*
CodeGuide	Omnicore	IDE	*www.omnicore.com*
Eclipse		IDE	*www.eclipse.org*
Idea	IntelliJ	IDE	*www.intellij.com*
JavaRefactor		Plugin for jEdit	*plugins.jedit.org/plugins/?JavaRefactor*
JBuilder	Borland	IDE	*www.borland.com/jbuilder*
JFactor	Instantiations	Plugin for JBuilder and VisualAge	*www.instantiations.com/jfactor*
JRefactory		Plugin for Elixir, JBuilder, and NetBeans.	*jrefactory.sourceforge.net*
RefactorIt	Aqris	Plugin for JBuilder, JDeveloper, NetBeans, and Sun ONE Studio	*www.refactorit.com*
Transmogrify		Plugin for JBuilder and Forte4Java	*transmogrify.sourceforge.net*
XRefactory	Xref-Tech	Plugin for Emacs, jEdit, and XEmacs	*www.xref-tech.com*

There is a tool list at *www.refactoring.com/tools.html* that includes these tools, as well as tools for several other languages.

APPENDIX C
INVERSES FOR REFACTORINGS

REFACTORING	INVERSE
Add Parameter	*Remove Parameter*
Change Bidirectional Association to Unidirectional	*Change Unidirectional Assocation to Bidirectional*
Change Reference to Value	*Change Value to Reference*
Change Unidirectional Association to Bidirectional	*Change Bidirectional Association to Unidirectional*
Change Value to Reference	*Change Reference to Value*
Collapse Hierarchy	*Extract Subclass*
Extract Class	*Inline Class*
Extract Method	*Inline Method*
Extract Subclass	*Collapse Hierarchy*
Hide Delegate	*Remove Middle Man*
Inline Class	*Extract Class*
Inline Method	*Extract Method*
Inline Temp	*Introduce Explaining Variable*
Introduce Explaining Variable	*Inline Temp*
Move Field	*Move Field*
Move Method	*Move Method*
Parameterize Method	*Replace Parameter with Explicit Methods*
Pull Up Field	*Push Down Field*
Pull Up Method	*Push Down Method*
Push Down Field	*Pull Up Field*

REFACTORING	INVERSE
Push Down Method	Pull Up Method
Remove Middle Man	Hide Delegate
Remove Parameter	Add Parameter
Rename Method	Rename Method
Replace Delegation with Inheritance	Replace Inheritance with Delegation
Replace Inheritance with Delegation	Replace Delegation with Inheritance
Replace Parameter with Explicit Methods	Parameterize Method
Substitute Algorithm	Substitute Algorithm

APPENDIX D
KEY REFACTORINGS

These UML diagrams are before-and-after representations for some important refactorings. See Fowler et al., *Refactoring: Improving the Design of Existing Code,* for a full catalog of transformations and the steps that will let you safely apply them.

Change Bidirectional Association to Unidirectional

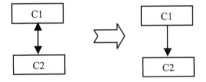

Duplicate Observed Data

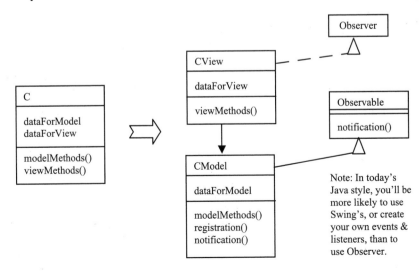

Extract Class

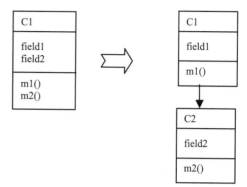

Extract Method

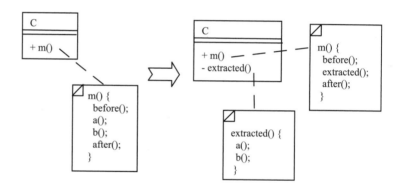

Move Field

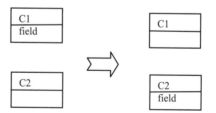

Move Method

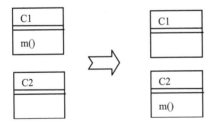

Replace Type Code with State/Strategy

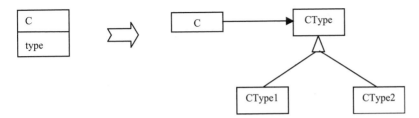

BIBLIOGRAPHY

Astels, Dave. *Test-Driven Development: A Practical Guide* (Upper Saddle River, NJ: Prentice Hall, 2003).

Beck, Kent. *Extreme Programming Explained: Embrace Change* (Boston: Addison-Wesley, 2000).

———. *Test-Driven Development: By Example* (Boston: Addison-Wesley, 2003).

Bentley, Jon. *More Programming Pearls* (Reading, MA: Addison-Wesley, 1988).

———. *Programming Pearls* (Reading, MA: Addison-Wesley, 1986).

———. *Writing Efficient Programs* (Upper Saddle River, NJ: Prentice Hall, 1982).

Cunningham, Ward. CRC Cards. *Portland Pattern Repository.* June 24, 2003. <http://c2.com/cgi/wiki?CrcCards>.

———. A CRC Description of HotDraw. *Portland Pattern Repository.* 1994. <http://www.c2.com/doc/crc/draw.html>.

Flanagan, David. *Java in a Nutshell, 4/e* (Sebastopol, CA: O'Reilly, 2002).

Fowler, Martin, et al. *Refactoring: Improving the Design of Existing Code* (Boston: Addison-Wesley, 2000).

Fowler, Martin, and Kendall Scott. *UML Distilled* (Reading, MA: Addison-Wesley, 1997).

Gamma, Erich, et al. *Design Patterns* (Reading, MA: Addison-Wesley, 1995).

Hunt, Andrew, and David Thomas. *The Pragmatic Programmer* (Boston: Addison-Wesley, 2000).

Jensen, Bill. *Simplicity: The New Competitive Advantage* (Cambridge, MA: Perseus Books, 2000).

Kent, William. "A Simple Guide to Five Normal Forms in Relational Theory," *Communications of the ACM* 26, no. 2 (February 1983), pp. 120–25.

Kernighan, Brian W., and P. J. Plauger. *The Elements of Programming Style* (New York: The McGraw-Hill Companies, 1988).

Martin, Robert C. *Agile Software Development: Principles, Patterns, and Practices* (Upper Saddle River, NJ: Prentice Hall, 2002).

Metsker, Steve. *Design Patterns Java Workbook* (Boston: Addison-Wesley, 2002).

Meyer, Bertrand. *Object-Oriented Software Construction* (Upper Saddle River, NJ: Prentice Hall, 1988).

Wake, William C. *Extreme Programming Explored* (Boston: Addison-Wesley, 2002).

INDEX

A

Alternative Classes with Different Interfaces, 54–55
    Extract Superclass Method and, 54
    Parameterize Method and, 54
    Rename Method and, 54

B

Background.java file (planning game simulator), 164
balance point, refactoring and, 8
bases, 13–14
Beck, Kent, 7, 10
behavior, objects, data and, 75
behavioral patterns, 72
Boolean conditions, Complicated Boolean Expression, 65–66

C

Card.java file (planning game simulator), 165–167
Catalog
    Catalog.itemsMatching(query), 151–154
    introduction, 151
    Process(catalog.data, query.data), 156–157
    Query.matchesIn(catalog), 155–156
Catalog.itemsMatching(query), 151–154
challenges
    description, 1–2
    refactoring cycle, 15
    tips for approaching, 3
Change Bidirectional Reference to Unidirectional, Inappropriate Intimacy (general form), 95
Changes, smells related to
    Combinatorial Explosion, 109–110

Divergent Change, 103–104
    Parallel Inheritance Hierarchies, 108–109
    Shotgun Surgery, 107–108
Classes, smells related to
    Data Class, 79–83
    Dead Code, 45
    Divergent Change, 103–104
    Incomplete Library Class, 111–116
    inheritance, 87
    Large Class, 25–26
        exercises, 26–30
        Extract Class, 26
        Extract Interface, 26
        Extract Subclass, 26
    Primitive Obsession and, 76
    Speculative Generality, 46
code
    code-based exercises, 2
    Dead code, 45–46
coding standards, names and, 39
Collapse Hierarchy
    Lazy Class and, 91
    Speculative Generality and, 47
Columbo syndrome (long methods), 20–25
Combinatorial Explosion, 109–110
Comments, 36
    exercises, 19–20
    Extract Method, 18
    Introduce Assertion, 18
    Rename Method, 18
    symptoms, 18
complexity
    Dead Code, 45–46
    exercises, 47–48

Complicated Boolean Expression, 65–66
conditional logic
    Complicated Boolean Expression, 65–66
    expressions, 66–67
    introduction, 63
    Null Check, 63–65
    Simulated Inheritance, 68–69
    Special Case, 67
    switch statements, 68–69
configuration management, 11
constants
    game, 145
    Magic Number smell, 52
contraindications, 1
control parameters, 30
Course.java file (database example), 122–124
CRC cards, 11
CRC (Class-Responsibility-Collaborator), 11
creational patterns, 71
Cunningham, Ward, 10
    names and, 39

D

data
    definition, 75
    objects, behavior and, 75
    Primitive Obsession, 75–79
Data Class, 36, 79–83
Data Clump, 36, 83–84
data smells, 75, 122
    Data Class, 79–80
    Data Clump, 83–84
    Primitive Obsession, 75–77
    Temporary Field, 84–85
databases, 121
    Course.java file, 122–124
    exercises, 135–139
    JDBC Database Access, 122
    Offering.java file, 124–126
    Reggie, 121
    Report.java file, 129–130
    Schedule.java file, 126–129
    TestReport.java file, 133–135
    TestSchedule.java file, 131–133
Dead Code, 45–46
    Speculative Generality and, 46

Decompose Conditional, Complicated Boolean Expression and, 65–66
defactoring, 182–183
DeMorgan's Law, Complicated Boolean Expression and, 65
design
    design patterns, interlude 3, 71–72
    emergent, 8
    refactoring and, 7
    up-front, 8
development episodes, game, 147–150
Divergent Change, 36, 103–107
Duplicated Code, 36, 53–54
    easy form, 53
    Extract Class and, 53
    Extract Method, 53
    Form Template Method and, 53
    hard form, 53
    Pull Up Field and, 53
    Pull Up Method and, 53
    Substitute Algorithm and, 54
duplication
    Alternative Classes with Different Interfaces, 54–55
    Combinatorial Explosion and, 110
    Duplicated Code, 53–54
    exercises, 55–61
    introduction, 51
    Magic Number, 52–53
    modules and, 51
    planning game simulator and, 173–176
    problems caused by, 51
    Shotgun Surgery, 107–108

E

Eiffel language, Inconsistent Names and, 43
embedded type names, 40–41
emergent design, refactoring and, 8
Encapsulate Collection, Data Class and, 79
Encapsulate Fields, 12
    Data Class and, 79
environment for refactoring, 11
exercises
    Catalog, 152
    code-based, 2
    comments, 19–20
    complexity, 47–48
    conditional logic

Complicated Boolean Expression, 66–67
Null Object, 64–65
Switch statements, 69–70
Data Class, 80–83
database example, 135–139
Divergent Change, 104–107
duplication, 55–61
Feature Envy, 94
further study, 182–183
game
changes, 143
Fuse Loops, 144
smells identification, 143
Incomplete Library Class, 112
large classes, 26–30
Lazy Class and, 91–92
library classes, 80–81
long methods, 21–25
long parameter list, 31–33
Middle Man and, 98–101
names, 43–44
planning game simulator, 168–170, 177–179
Primitive Obsession, 77–79
Query, 152
Refused Bequest and, 89–90
solutions, 2
Extract Class
Data Clump and, 84
Divergent Change, 104
Duplicated Code and, 53
Inappropriate Intimacy (general form), 95
large classes, 26
Shotgun Surgery, 107
Temporary Field and, 85
Extract Interface, large classes, 26
Extract Method
comment blocks, 18
Data Class and, 80
Duplicated Code, 53
Feature Envy and, 94
long methods, 21
Message Chains and, 96
Query and, 153
Switch statements, 68
Extract Subclass
Divergent Change, 104
large classes, 26
Refused Bequest and, 88

Extract Superclass
Alternative Classes with Different Interfaces, 54
Divergent Change, 104
Query, 153
Extreme Programming. *See* XP (Extreme Programming)

F

Feature Envy, 36, 93–95
Duplicated Code and, 53
fields
Dead Code, 45
Speculative Generality, 46
Form Template Method
Duplicated Code and, 53
Inappropriate Intimacy and (subclass form), 90
Fowler, Martin, 10
Fowler's *Refactoring*, 1
Fuse Loops, game exercise, 144

G

game. *See also* planning game simulator
changes, 143
code, 141–143
constants, 145
development episodes, 147–150
exercises
Fuse Loops, 144
smells identification, 143
iterators, 146–147
for loops, 143–144
magic numbers, 145
subjunctive programming, 146
test-driven design, 141
Gen-A-Refactoring, 117
getter methods, creating, 12–13
Gorts, Sven, 7

H

Hide Delegate
Inappropriate Intimacy (general form), 95
Message Chains, 96
Hide Method, public methods, 13
hierarchies, Parallel Inheritance Hierarchies, 108–109
Hungarian notation, Type Embedded in Name smell, 40

I

IDE (Integrated Development Environment), 11
if statements, conditional logic and, 67
Inappropriate Intimacy, 36
   general form, 95
   subclass form, 90
Incomplete Library Class, 36, 111–116
Inconsistent Names, 42–44
inheritance
   Inappropriate Intimacy (subclass form), 90
   introduction, 87
   Lazy Class, 90–92
   Refused Bequest and, 87–90
Inline Class
   Shotgun Surgery, 107
   Speculative Generality and, 47
Inline Method, Speculative Generality and, 47
instance variables, large classes, 25
integers, Primitive Obsession and, 75–76
interfaces, Extract Interface, 26
interludes
   design patterns, 71–72
   Gen-A-Refactoring, 117
   inverses, 49–50
   smells and refactorings, 35–37
interruption points, 13–14
Introduce Assertion, comments, 18
Introduce Explaining Variable, Complicated Boolean
  Expression and, 65–66
Introduce Foreign Method, Incomplete Library Class, 112
Introduce Local Extension, Incomplete Library Class, 112
Introduce Null Object, conditional logic, 64
Introduce Parameter Object, Data Clump and, 84
inverses of refactorings, 49–50

J

Java Tutorial, 122
JDBC Database Access, 122. *See also* Java Tutorial
JDBC Short Course, 122–137
Johnson, Ralph, 10
JUnit test framework, 11

K

kata, 183

L

Large Class, 36
   exercises, 26–30
   Extract Class, 26
   Extract Interface, 26
   Extract Subclass, 26
   symptoms, 25
Lazy Class, 36, 90–92
length metrics, 2
library classes
   exercises, 80–81
   Incomplete Library Class, 111–116
lines, large classes, 25
listings
   refactorings, 37
   smells, 38
Long Method, 36
   exercises, 21–25
   Extract Method, 21
   symptoms, 20
Long Parameter List, 36
   symptoms, 30

M

Magic Number, 52–53
making numbers, metrics and, 17
malfactoring, 182–183
Message Chains, 36, 96
methods
   Dead Code, 45
   getter, creating, 12–13
   Hide Method, 13
   Large Class, 25
   Long Method, 20–25
   parameters, replacing, 30
   setter, creating, 12–13
   Speculative Generality, 46
metrics
   length metrics, 2, 17
   making numbers, 17
   smells, catching, 17
Middle Man, 36, 97–101
modules, duplication and, 51
Move Field
   Inappropriate Intimacy (general form), 95
   Parallel Inheritance Hierarchies, 108
   Shotgun Surgery, 107

Move Method
    Data Clump and, 84
    Feature Envy and, 94
    Inappropriate Intimacy (general form), 95
    Message Chains and, 96
    Parallel Inheritance Hierarchies, 108
    Shotgun Surgery, 107
    Switch statements, 68

N

names
    coding standards and, 39
    Cunningham, Ward, 39
    exercises, 43–44
    naming standards, 39
    Type Embedded in Name (Including Hungarian), 40–41
near-primitive types, Primitive Obsession and, 75–76
nouns, 117
Null Check, 63–65

O

OAOO (once and only once), 10
objects
    coupling, long parameter lists, 30
    data, behavior and, 75
    missing, Primitive Obsession and, 76
Offering.java file (database example), 124–126
OrQuery class, 153

P

Parallel Inheritance Hierarchies, 36, 108–109
Parameterize Method, Alternative Classes with Different Interfaces, 54
parameters
    control parameters, 30
    Dead Code, 45
    Long Parameter List, 30–33
    methods, replacing with, 30
    Speculative Generality, 46
Parnas, David (information hiding), 51
partners, 11
patterns
    behaviorial patterns, 72

    creational patterns, 71
    design patterns, 71–72
    structural patterns, 71
payoff, 1
performance, 154
planning game simulator
    Background class, 159
    Background.java file, 164
    Card class, 159
    Card.java file, 165–167
    duplication and, 173–176
    exercises, 177–179
    redistributing features, 170–173
    selection troubles, 173–176
    Table class, 159
    Table.java file, 160–164
    velocity updates, 176
PlanningGame class, 170
The Pragmatic Programmer, 96
Preserve Whole Object, Data Clump and, 84
Primitive Obsession, 36
    data and, 75–79
    exercises, 77–79
primitive types, Primitive Obsession and, 75–76
Process(catalog.data, query.data), 156–157
programming, subjunctive programming, 146
public methods, making private, 13
Pull Up Field, Duplicated Code and, 53
Pull Up Method, Duplicated Code and, 53
Push Down Field, Refused Bequest and, 88
Push Down Method, Refused Bequest and, 88

Q

Query
    Catalog.itemsMatching(query), 151–154
    Extract Method, 153
    Extract Superclass, 153
    introduction, 151
    OrQuery class, 153
    Process(catalog.data, query.data), 156–157
Query.matchesIn(catalog), 155–156

R

redistributing features, planning game simulator, 170–173

refactoring
    definition, 7–8
    environment for, 11
    finishing, 9–10
    size, 8
    XP and, 10
refactoring cycle
    challenges, 15
    pattern, 9
refactorings list, 37
    inverses, 49–50
references
    calls, replacing with, 13
    replacing, 14
Refused Bequest, 36, 87–90
Reggie, 121
Remove Method, Speculative Generality and, 47
Remove Middle Man, 97
Remove Parameter, Speculative Generality and, 47
Remove Setting Methods, Data Class and, 79
Rename Method
    Alternative Classes with Different Interfaces, 54
    comments, 18
    Inconsistent Names, 43
    Type Embedded in Name (Including Hungarian), 41
    Uncommunicative Name, 41–42
Replace Array with Object, Primitive Obsession and, 76
Replace Conditional with Polymorphism
    Primitive Obsession and, 76
    Special Case and, 67
    Switch statements, 68
Replace Delegation with Inheritance, Middle Man and, 97
Replace Inheritance with Delegation
    Combinatorial Explosion, 109–110
    Inappropriate Intimacy and (subclass form), 90
    Inappropriate Intimacy (general form), 95
    Refused Bequest and, 88
Replace Magic Number with Symbolic Constant, 52
Replace Parameter with Method, 30
Replace Type Code with Class, Primitive Obsession and, 76
Replace Type Code with State/Strategy
    Primitive Obsession and, 76
    Switch statements, 68
Replace Type Code with Subclass
    Primitive Obsession and, 76
    switch statements, 68
replacing
    calls, with references, 13

parameters with methods, 30
    references, 14
Report.java file (database example), 129–130
resources, Web sites, 183
responsibility
    Feature Envy, 93–95
    Inappropriate Intimacy (general form), 95
    introduction, 93
    Message Chains, 96
    Middle Man, 97–101

S

safe points, 13–14
Schedule.java file (database example), 126–129
Self Encapsulate Field
    Inappropriate Intimacy and (subclass form), 90
    Inappropriate Intimacy (general form), 95
setter methods, creating, 12–13
Shotgun Surgery, 36, 107–108
Simulated Inheritance, 68–70
smells
    Alternative Classes with Different Interfaces, 36
    causes, 1
    between classes, 2
    within classes, 2
    Comments, 18–20, 36
    Data Class, 36
    Data Clump, 36
    data smells, 122
    Dead Code, 45–46
    definition, 1
    description, 8–9
    Divergent Change, 36
    Duplicated Code, 36
    Feature Envy, 36
    Inappropriate Intimacy, 36
    Incomplete Library Class, 36
    Inconsistent Names, 42–44
    Large Class, 36
    Lazy Class, 36
    length metrics, 2
    listing, 38
    Long Class, 25–30
    Long Method, 20–25, 36
    Long Parameter List, 30–33, 36
    Magic Number, 52–53
    Message Chains, 36

Middle Man, 36
Parallel Inheritance Hierarchies, 36
Primitive Obsession, 36
refactorings list, 36
Refused Bequest, 36
Shotgun Surgery, 36
Special Case, 67
Speculative Generality, 36, 46–47
Switch Statements, 36
symptoms, 1
Temporary Field, 36
Type Embedded in Name (Including Hungarian), 40
Uncommunicative Name, 41–42
Special Case, 67
Speculative Generality, 36, 46–47
Dead Code and, 46
steps of refactoring, 12
strings, constants, Primitive Obsession and, 75–76
structural patterns, 71
subclasses
Extract Subclass, large classes, 26
superclasses, 2
subjunctive programming, 146
Substitute Algorithm, Duplicated Code and, 54
superclasses, subclasses and, 2
Switch Statements, 36
conditional logic, 68–69
exercises, 69–70
symptoms of smells, 1

T

Table.java file (planning game simulator), 160–164
teams, 11
Tease Apart Inheritance, Combinatorial Explosion, 110

Temporary Field, 36, 84–85
TestCase class, 11
test-driven development, 10
game, 141
testing, 11, 13–14, 181–182
TestReport.java file (database example), 133–135
tests, JUnit test framework, 11
TestSchedule.java file (database example), 131–133
transformations, safe, 12
Type Embedded in Name (Including Hungarian), symptoms, 40
types, simulated, Primitive Obsession and, 76

U

UML (Unified Modeling Language), sketches, 11
Uncommunicative Name, 41–42
up-front design, refactoring and, 8

V

variables, Dead Code, 45
velocity updates, 176
verb noun format, 117
verbs, 117
version control, 11

W

Web site resources, 183

X

XP (Extreme Programming), refactoring and, 7, 10